MIDDLE SCHOOL SPELLING & VOCABULARY WORKBOOK

SPELLING AND VOCABULARY GRADE 6,7 & 8: ACHIEVE HIGHER TEST SCORES WITH INTERACTIVE EXERCISES

DR. FANATOMY

copyright@ dr. fanatomy 2024

All rights reserved. No part of this publication may be reproduced, distributed, or transmitted in any form or by any means, including photocopying, recording, or other electronic or mechanical methods, without the prior written permission of the publisher, except in the case of brief quotations embodied in critical reviews and certain other noncommercial uses permitted by copyright law.

This book is a work of non-fiction, and any resemblance to actual persons, living or dead, or actual events is purely coincidental.

The information and techniques described in this book are intended for educational and informational purposes only. The author and publisher shall not be held liable for any injury, damage, or loss arising from using or misusing the information presented in this book.

While every effort has been made to ensure the accuracy of the information contained within this book, the author and publisher make no warranties or representations express or implied, about the completeness, accuracy, reliability, suitability, or availability with respect to the contents of this book for any purpose. The use of any information provided in this book is at the reader's own risk.

Bonus Booklet For You!

With great pleasure, I warmly welcome you to purchase the book. Congratulations on stepping towards improving yourself and developing the skills necessary to thrive as a teenager and beyond.

Below is a surprise gift for you!

Download it from the link (or scan the QR code below)
https://bit.ly/TeeNavigationBonus

"29" LIFE SECRETS FOR TEENS YOU'LL ONLY DISCOVER WHEN YOU TURN 25!

DR. FANATOMY

TABLE OF CONTENTS

1. INTRODUCTION TO SPELLING AND VOCABULARY (Pg:4-17)

- Why Spelling and Vocabulary Matter
- Table: Spelling Mistakes and Their Impact
- Benefits for School Success and Beyond
- Common Spelling and Vocabulary Challenges in Middle School
- Overcoming Mispronunciations and Spelling Errors
- Tip for Success:
- Fun Facts About Words Middle Schoolers Commonly Misspell
- Basic Vocabulary Table: Subject Wise
- Trivia Corner
- Activity Corner 1

2. BUILDING A STRONG VOCABULARY FOUNDATION (Pg: 18-24)

- Developing Middle School-Level Vocabulary
- Vocabulary Building Techniques
- Using Context Clues
- Unlocking the Power of Prefixes and Suffixes
- Trivia Corner
- Activity Corner 2

3. MASTERING SPELLING RULES (Pg: 25 - 32)

- Essential Spelling Rules
- Understanding Vowel and Consonant Patterns
- Common Spelling Challenges
- Managing Double Letters and Silent Letters
- Breaking Down Compound Words
- Trivia Corner
- Activity Corner 3

4. VOCABULARY IN EVERYDAY LIFE (Pg: 33-41)

- Vocabulary in Everyday Life
- What is Vocabulary?
- How Can You Use Vocabulary in Everyday Life?
- Applying Vocabulary in Everyday Context
- Synonyms, Antonyms, and Homophones
- Finding the Right Word for the Right Situation
- Trivia Corner
- Activity Corner 4

5. READING FOR VOCABULARY GROWTH (Pg: 42 - 53)

- Reading Strategies for Vocabulary Growth
- How Reading Expands Your Vocabulary
- Reading Context Table
- Choosing Books and Articles at Your Grade Level
- Highlighting and Defining New Words
- Practice Exercises with Short Reading Passages
- Fun Facts About Words First Seen in Famous Books
- Create a Reading Vocabulary Journal
- Table: Context Clues in Reading

- *Table: Defining New Words with Example Sentences*
- *Table: Challenging Vocabulary from Books*
- *Table: Annotating Vocabulary in Context*
- *Table: Practice Exercise with Context Clues*
- *Trivia Corner*
- *Activity Corner 5*

6. WORD ROOTS, PREFIXES, AND SUFFIXES (Pg: 54-61)

- *Introduction to Roots, Prefixes, and Suffixes*
- *Latin and Greek Roots Common in Middle School Words*
- *Expanding Vocabulary with Affixes*
- *How Latin and Greek Roots Shape Everyday English*
- *Build Your Word Trees with Roots and Affixes*
- *Table of prefixes and suffixes*
- *Trivia Corner*
- *Activity Corner 6*

7. SPELLING WITH CONFIDENCE: A FUN AND CHALLENGING ADVENTURE (Pg: 62-68)

- *Tackling Tricky Words: A Spelling Safari*
- *Multisyllabic Mastery: Breaking Down Words*
- *Homophone Heroes: Choosing the Right Word*
- *Memory Magic: Mnemonics and Visualization*
- *50 Commonly Misspelled Words and Tricks to Remember Them*
- *Trivia Corner*
- *Activity Corner 7*

8. VOCABULARY IN WRITING (Pg: 69-79)

- *Boosting Your Writing with Strong Vocabulary*
- *Transitioning from Simple Words to Richer Vocabulary*
- *Example Table: Word Transition*
- *Avoiding Repetitive Words*
- *Using a Thesaurus Effectively*
- *Practice Exercises on Integrating Vocabulary in Writing*
- *Example Table: Simple vs. Strong Vocabulary*
- *Example Table: Word Transitions*
- *Example Table: Before and After*
- *Example Table: Using a Thesaurus Correctly*
- *Trivia Corner*
- *Activity Corner 8*

9. PROOFREADING FOR SPELLING AND VOCABULARY ERRORS (Pg: 80-88)

- *Introduction*
- *Techniques for Catching Spelling Mistakes*
- *Using Technology to Help Proofread*
- *Editing Your Work*
- *Spotting Vocabulary and Grammar Errors*
- *Common Homophones Table*
- *Table: Common spelling and vocabulary errors*
- *Trivia Corner*
- *Activity Corner 9*

10. REAL-WORLD USES OF SPELLING AND VOCABULARY SKILLS
(Pg: 89 - 95)

- *How Spelling and Vocabulary Help in School*
- *Practical Applications for Future Success*
- *Table: Improving Sentences for Job Applications*
- *Letters, Emails, and Online Communication*
- *Example: Sending an Email*
- *Table: Informal vs. Formal Communication*
- *Writing Emails and Letters with Proper Vocabulary*
- *Letter Example:*
- *Trivia Corner*
- *Activity Corner 10*

ACTIVITY ANSWERS
(Pg: 96 -105)

11. BUILD YOUR WORD BANK: VOCABULARY ESSENTIALS
(Pg: 106 - 113)

Table: Vocabulary Improvement Groups
Group 1: Words from Latin Roots
Group 2: Words from Greek Roots
Group 3: Words with Positive Connotations
Group 4: Words with Negative Connotations
Group 5: Academic Words

Table: Most Used Root Words from Different Languages
Table 1: Latin Roots
Table 2: Greek Roots
Table 3: French and Sanskrit Roots
Table 4: German Roots
Table 5: Old English Roots

12. MOST MISSPELLED WORDS & TRICKS TO REMEMBER
(Pg: 114 -116)

CONCLUSION
(Pg: 117)

APPENDIX
(Pg: 118 -120)

- *Appendix- 1: Additional Resources*
- *Appendix- 2: Writing Prompts to Use New Vocabulary in Context*

1. Introduction to Spelling and Vocabulary

Why Spelling and Vocabulary Matter

Words are your secret weapons. They help you communicate, express yourself, and impress others. Whether chatting with friends, answering questions in class, or writing an essay, using the right words makes a huge difference. The more precise you are, the better people will understand you.

Table: Spelling Mistakes and Their Impact

Incorrect Sentence	Correct Sentence	Why It Matters
I'm defiantly going to the game.	I'm definitely going to the game.	"Defiantly" means to rebel, not the same as "definitely!"
He there new here.	He they're new here.	Using the wrong word confuses the meaning.

Example:

Imagine writing "I'm **defiantly** going to the game" when you meant "**definitely**." That small mistake completely changes the meaning! Proper spelling avoids these misunderstandings.

Let's take a fun scenario:

Imagine you're explaining a hilarious joke to your friend, but instead of using the right words, you fumble around, trying to make sense of it.

- Incorrect: "That movie was like, so, um, good, I guess."
- Correct: "That movie was incredible! I laughed so hard."

See the difference? The right words can make what you say sound stronger and clearer. Words matter whether it's making your friend laugh, impressing your teacher, or getting your point across in an argument!

Real-Life Example:

- Incorrect: "That dog was real big."
- Correct: "That dog was enormous!"

Choosing better words makes your descriptions more vivid, helping your audience picture precisely what you mean. Using varied vocabulary also makes your writing more enjoyable!

Benefits for School Success and Beyond

Mastering spelling and vocabulary is like leveling up your game in every subject, not just English. When you can spell well and use a wide range of vocabulary, it benefits your performance across subjects like science, social studies, and even math.

Words like "photosynthesis" in science or "revolution" in history suddenly become more accessible to understand and spell correctly. Improving your vocabulary makes reading more straightforward, so you'll also perform better on tests, assignments, and exams. Beyond school, strong spelling and vocabulary skills can help you land jobs, write effective emails, and build a strong social media presence!

Subject	Key Vocabulary Words	Spelling Example
Science	Photosynthesis, Molecule	Photosynthesis
Math	Equation, Hypothesis	Equation
Social Studies	Democracy, Civilization	Democracy
English	Narrative, Metaphor	Narrative

Mastering these words helps you excel across multiple subjects. The better you understand and spell these words, the easier it will be to succeed in all your classes.

Area	Benefit	Example
School	Better grades on tests and essays	Correctly spelling difficult words in essays improves grades.
Reading	Easier understanding of books and articles	Knowing the meaning of new words helps you enjoy reading more.
Communication	Clearer speech and writing	Using the right words makes your ideas easier to understand.
Future Careers	Better opportunities in jobs and college	Employers value good writing and communication skills.

Common Spelling and Vocabulary Challenges in Middle School

As you progress through middle school, you'll find that the words you come across become longer, more complex, and sometimes trickier to spell and understand. However, there's no need to worry!

Many students encounter similar challenges, and by acknowledging them, you'll be better prepared to overcome them. Below, you'll find some of the most common spelling and vocabulary difficulties you might encounter:

- **Pronunciation Mismatches:**

Sometimes, words don't sound how they're spelled, leading to confusion.
Example: "February" is often pronounced "Febuary," which can cause students to misspell it.

- **Remembering Meanings:**

When learning new vocabulary in subjects like science, social studies, or literature, it can be easy to forget what words mean if you don't practice using them regularly.
Example: You might come across the word "photosynthesis" in science class but forget its meaning unless you revisit it in context.

- **Silent Letters:**

Some words have letters that aren't pronounced, making them easy to miss when spelling.
Example: In the word "knight," the "k" is silent, yet it must be included in the spelling.

- **Homophones:**

Homophones are words that sound alike but have different meanings and spellings, which can make them confusing.
Example: Words like "their," "there," and "they're" sound the same, but their meanings are different.

- **Long Words:**

Due to their length and complexity, longer words can be challenging, especially when they contain double letters or follow unusual spelling rules.
Example: Words like "embarrassment" and "independent" can be tricky because they are long and repeat letters.

Overcoming Mispronunciations and Spelling Errors

One of the best ways to improve your spelling is to break words down into smaller parts or syllables. This helps make complicated words easier to remember. Another useful strategy is creating mnemonic devices—tricks that help you recall tricky spellings.

Example of Syllable Breakdown:

- February: Feb-ru-ar-y (4 syllables)
- Photosynthesis: Pho-to-syn-the-sis (5 syllables)

Mnemonic Example: To remember how to spell "necessary," you could use the phrase:

"Never Eat Cream, Eat Salad Sandwiches And Rare Yams" (N-E-C-E-S-S-A-R-Y).

Every time you write "necessary," you'll have this sentence to remind you of the correct spelling.

Word	Syllable Breakdown	Practice Saying and Spelling
Environment	En-vi-ron-ment	Break it down and practice each part slowly.
Necessary	Nec-es-sa-ry	Repeat the syllables out loud to memorize them.
Restaurant	Res-tau-rant	Say it a few times to get comfortable with the word.

Tip for Success:

Breaking down difficult words into smaller syllables, like "nec-es-sa-ry" for "necessary," helps you remember and spell them correctly.

Fun Facts About Words Middle Schoolers Commonly Misspell

Word	Common Mistake	Fun Fact
Misspell	Only one "s"	Ironically, "misspell" is often misspelled!
Definitely	Mixed up with "defiantly"	Many people confuse these two because they sound similar.
Embarrassment	Missing a letter	The double "r" and "s" make this word especially tricky.

Basic Vocabulary: Subject Wise

Science

Word	Meaning	Example Sentence
Photosynthesis	Process by which plants make food using sunlight	Plants rely on photosynthesis to convert sunlight into energy.
Molecule	A group of atoms bonded together	Water is made up of two hydrogen molecules and one oxygen molecule.
Gravity	The force that attracts objects toward Earth	Gravity keeps us from floating off the ground.
Atom	The smallest unit of a chemical element	Everything around us is made up of tiny atoms.
Ecosystem	A biological community of interacting organisms	The forest is a delicate ecosystem with many living organisms.
Hypothesis	A proposed explanation for a phenomenon	Our science experiment started with a hypothesis about plant growth.
Erosion	The process by which earth is worn away by natural forces	The coastline is shrinking due to erosion caused by waves.
Osmosis	Movement of water molecules through a membrane	Plants absorb water through osmosis in their roots.
Inertia	A tendency to remain unchanged or resist movement	Inertia causes the object to stay still until force is applied.
Biodiversity	The variety of life in a particular habitat or ecosystem	Protecting biodiversity ensures the survival of various species.

Basic Vocabulary: Subject Wise

Science

Word	Meaning	Example Sentence
Photosynthesis	Process by which plants make food using sunlight	Plants rely on photosynthesis to convert sunlight into energy.
Molecule	A group of atoms bonded together	Water is made up of two hydrogen molecules and one oxygen molecule.
Gravity	The force that attracts objects toward Earth	Gravity keeps us from floating off the ground.
Atom	The smallest unit of a chemical element	Everything around us is made up of tiny atoms.
Ecosystem	A biological community of interacting organisms	The forest is a delicate ecosystem with many living organisms.
Hypothesis	A proposed explanation for a phenomenon	Our science experiment started with a hypothesis about plant growth.
Erosion	The process by which earth is worn away by natural forces	The coastline is shrinking due to erosion caused by waves.
Osmosis	Movement of water molecules through a membrane	Plants absorb water through osmosis in their roots.
Inertia	A tendency to remain unchanged or resist movement	Inertia causes the object to stay still until force is applied.
Biodiversity	The variety of life in a particular habitat or ecosystem	Protecting biodiversity ensures the survival of various species.

Basic Vocabulary: Subject Wise

Math

Word	Meaning	Example Sentence
Equation	A mathematical statement that asserts equality	Solve the equation to find the value of 'x'.
Diameter	A straight line passing through the center of a circle	The diameter of the circle measures 10 inches.
Fraction	A numerical quantity that is not a whole number	We learned how to add and subtract fractions in math class.
Perimeter	The distance around a figure or shape	We calculated the perimeter of the rectangle during class.
Probability	The likelihood of something happening	The probability of rolling a six on a die is one in six.
Geometry	The branch of mathematics concerning shapes and spaces	We studied the basics of geometry by drawing triangles.
Hypotenuse	The longest side of a right triangle	The hypotenuse is always opposite the right angle.
Algorithm	A step-by-step procedure for solving a problem	We used an algorithm to solve the complicated equation.
Variable	A symbol used to represent a number	In algebra, 'x' is often used as a variable.
Quadrilateral	A four-sided polygon	A square is a type of quadrilateral with equal sides.

Basic Vocabulary: Subject Wise

Social Studies

Word	Meaning	Example Sentence
Democracy	A system of government by the whole population	In a democracy, citizens have the power to vote for their leaders.
Revolution	A dramatic change in political power	The American Revolution led to the birth of a new nation.
Civilization	An advanced state of human society	Ancient civilizations like Egypt and Mesopotamia developed along rivers.
Constitution	A set of principles or rules for governing a country	The U.S. Constitution outlines the rights and freedoms of citizens.
Economy	The system of production, distribution, and consumption	The country's economy relies on exports like oil and technology.
Monarchy	A form of government with a monarch at the head	In a monarchy, the king or queen has significant power.
Colonization	The establishment of control over indigenous people	Colonization had a lasting impact on the native cultures of America.
Treaty	A formal agreement between countries	The Treaty of Versailles ended World War I.
Artifact	An object made by a human being, typically of cultural interest	The museum displayed artifacts from ancient civilizations.
Segregation	The enforced separation of different racial groups	Segregation was a major issue during the Civil Rights Movement.

Basic Vocabulary: Subject Wise

English/Language Arts

Word	Meaning	Example Sentence
Narrative	A spoken or written account of connected events	The novel is a first-person narrative of the hero's journey.
Metaphor	A figure of speech that describes an object as something else	The phrase 'time is a thief' is an example of a metaphor.
Foreshadowing	A literary device that hints at future events	The storm in the first chapter foreshadows the conflict to come.
Simile	A figure of speech comparing two things using "like" or "as"	"She runs as fast as lightning," is a common simile.
Plot	The main events of a story	The plot of the mystery novel kept us guessing until the end.
Dialogue	The conversation between characters in a book, play, or movie	The dialogue between the two characters was witty and engaging.
Protagonist	The main character in a story	The protagonist of the novel embarks on a quest to find the lost treasure.
Genre	A category of artistic composition	Science fiction is my favorite literary genre.
Symbolism	The use of symbols to represent ideas or qualities	The rose in the poem is a symbol of love and beauty.
Alliteration	The occurrence of the same letter or sound at the beginning of adjacent words	Peter Piper picked a peck of pickled peppers is an example of alliteration.

Basic Vocabulary: Subject Wise

Physical Education

Word	Meaning	Example Sentence
Cardiovascular	Relating to the heart and blood vessels	Running is a great cardiovascular exercise to improve heart health.
Endurance	The ability to sustain prolonged physical activity	Athletes need endurance to compete in long-distance races.
Agility	The ability to move quickly and easily	Soccer players need agility to change direction on the field.
Flexibility	The quality of bending easily without breaking	Stretching helps improve flexibility and prevents injury.
Balance	The ability to maintain control of the body's position	Gymnasts need excellent balance to perform on the beam.
Coordination	The ability to use different parts of the body together smoothly	Good hand-eye coordination is essential in sports like tennis.
Hydration	The process of providing adequate water to the body	Hydration is crucial for athletes during intense training sessions.
Muscle	A tissue that contracts to produce movement	Lifting weights helps build muscle strength.
Stamina	The ability to sustain physical or mental effort	Building stamina allows you to exercise for longer periods.
Nutrition	The process of providing or obtaining the food necessary for health	Good nutrition is key to maintaining a healthy lifestyle.

Trivia Corner

- *"Ghost Letters" Exist:* The "k" is silent in the word knight. It's called a "ghost letter" because you don't hear it, but it's still there!

- *Most Commonly Misspelled Word:* One of the most commonly misspelled words in English is misspelled. It's ironic because people misspell "misspell" all the time!

- *Longest Word with One Vowel:* The longest word in English with only one vowel is strengths. It has eight letters but just one vowel—pretty cool, right?

- *The Shortest Complete Sentence:* Did you know the shortest complete sentence in English is just two letters? It's "Go!" A command counts as a full sentence!

- *The Word with the Most Definitions:* The word set has over 400 definitions in the dictionary. You could say it's pretty "set" in its ways!

- *Silent Letters Everywhere:* About 60% of English words contain silent letters! Words like thumb, honest, and lamb are just a few examples.

- *Palindromes Are Fun:* A palindrome is a word that reads the same forward and backward, like racecar or level. Try thinking of more!

- *Two Common Words with All Vowels:* Education and facetious are two of the few words that use all five vowels (a, e, i, o, u) in order!

- *Commonly Confused Homophones:* The word pairs "your" and "you're" are among the most commonly confused homophones in the English language. Pay attention to that apostrophe!

- *The Great Spelling Debate:* Americans spell it color, while the British spell it colour. Both are correct, depending on where you live!

ACTIVITY CORNER 1

Activity 1: Spelling Challenge

Correct the spelling errors in the following sentences.

Sentences:

1. The **recieve** for the project was not ready.
2. She had **definately** planned to attend the **comitee** meeting.
3. The **enviornment** club helped clean the park.

Activity 2: Choose the correct word

Choose the correct word from the list to complete each sentence.

Word List: (there, their, they're; accept, except; effect, affect)

Sentences:

1. The decision did not ___ the outcome.
2. Please ___ my apology for the delay.
3. ___ going to the park later this evening.

Activity 3: Homophones Match-Up activity

Words	Match the Correct Definition (A-F)
Principal	A. A polite expression of praise
Principle	B. The head of a school
Complement	C. Something that completes or enhances something else
Compliment	D. A rule or fundamental truth
Affect	E. To have an impact on something
Effect	F. A result or outcome

Activity 4: Match the Word to the Correct Meaning

Word	Meaning Options
Inevitable	a) Unavoidable b) Exciting c) Surprising
Precise	a) Careful b) Exact c) Late
Revolution	a) Sudden change b) Repeated action c) Calm situation
Molecule	a) Tiny particle b) Large object c) Medium-sized animal

2. Building a Strong Vocabulary Foundation

Developing Middle School-Level Vocabulary

Developing a robust vocabulary is akin to assembling a superhero's arsenal for your brain. The greater your word knowledge, the simpler it becomes to articulate your thoughts, compose creatively, and comprehend written material. As you progress through middle school, you are anticipated to utilize more sophisticated vocabulary. Instead of describing something as "good," consider using words like "fantastic" or "remarkable." This enhances the appeal of your writing and fosters a more assured tone!

Example:

- Instead of: "The pizza was good."
- Try: "The pizza was delicious and bursting with flavor!"

Vocabulary Building Techniques

Growing your vocabulary can be fun and doesn't have to feel like a chore. Here are some exciting techniques to help you become a word wizard:

- **Read Regularly**: The more you read, the more new words you'll encounter. Reading is a great way to discover new words, whether it's books, comics, magazines, or even blogs. When you find a word you don't know, jot it down and look it up!

- **Keep a Vocabulary Journal**: Write down new words, their meanings, and how to use them in sentences. This helps you remember and use the words in conversations or your writing.

Vocabulary Journal Example

Word	Meaning	Sentence
Ambitious	Having a strong desire to succeed	She is ambitious and works hard to achieve her goals.
Eager	Wanting to do something very much	He was eager to join the basketball team this year.
Enthusiastic	Showing intense excitement	She was enthusiastic about starting her science project.

- **Play Word Games:** Challenge yourself with word games like Scrabble and Boggle or apps like Vocabulary.com. You can even set up a friendly competition with your friends to see who can learn more words!

Using Context Clues

When you come across a word you don't know, don't panic! You can often figure out the meaning by looking at the other words around it—context clues. Let's explore some examples:

Example 1:

- Sentence: "The sky was so ominous, with dark clouds and thunder rumbling in the distance."
- Context Clue: The dark clouds and thunder suggest that "ominous" might mean something scary or threatening.

Example 2:

- Sentence: "The girl was elated after winning the spelling bee."
- Context Clue: Winning the spelling bee is a happy event, so "elated" likely means very happy.

Types of Context Clues

Type	Example
Definition	"The word 'gigantic' means something very large."
Synonym	"She was so jubilant, or extremely joyful, after hearing the good news."
Antonym	"Unlike his boisterous friends, Mark was quiet and reserved."
Inference	"She studied all night, so it's no surprise she excelled on the test."

Unlocking the Power of Prefixes and Suffixes

Prefixes and suffixes act as magic keys that help unlock the meaning of unfamiliar words. A prefix is added to the beginning of a word, while a suffix is added to the end. Understanding common prefixes and suffixes can aid in comprehending and deciphering unfamiliar words.

Common Prefixes:

Prefix	Meaning	Example	Explanation
Un-	Not	Unhappy	"Unhappy" means not happy.
Re-	Again	Rebuild	"Rebuild" means to build again.
Pre-	Before	Preheat	"Preheat" means to heat beforehand.

Common Suffixes:

Suffix	Meaning	Example	Explanation
-ful	Full of	Joyful	"Joyful" means full of joy.
-less	Without	Hopeless	"Hopeless" means without hope.
-ment	Action/Process	Excitement	"Excitement" refers to being excited.

Example:

Word: "Unstoppable"
- Prefix: Un- (meaning not)
- Root Word: Stop
- Suffix: -able (meaning capable of)
- Meaning: Not capable of being stopped.

By learning these building blocks, you'll be able to break down and understand words that seem tricky at first!

Trivia Corner

- The Longest Word in the Dictionary: Did you know that the longest word in the English dictionary is pneumonoultramicroscopicsilicovolcanoconiosis? It's a type of lung disease caused by inhaling very fine dust. Can you imagine spelling that in a competition?

- "E" is Everywhere: The most commonly used letter in the English language is E. About 11% of all written English words contain this letter!

- Word Origins from Animals: The word "zebra" comes from the Portuguese word zebra, meaning wild ass or horse. Many words we use today come from animal names!

- Palindromes are Word Fun: A palindrome is a word that reads the same forward and backward. Examples include "level," "madam," and "racecar." Can you think of more?

- Shakespeare the Wordsmith: William Shakespeare invented over 1,700 words that we still use today, including "eyeball," "swagger," and "lonely." Imagine coming up with that many words!

- Synonyms Galore: The word "run" has the most synonyms in the English language. You could say "dash," "jog," "sprint," "gallop," and so many more!

- Supercalifragilisticexpialidocious: This famous word from the Disney movie Mary Poppins is 34 letters long! It's often used to describe something fantastic or extraordinary.

- The Word "Goodbye": The word "goodbye" actually comes from the phrase "God be with ye" from centuries ago. It was shortened over time to the "goodbye" we use today.

- Silent "K" in Knighthood: In Old English, the "K" in words like "knight" and "knife" used to be pronounced! Over time, it became silent, but we still spell the words with the "K."

- The Alphabet's Orphan Letter: The letter "Q" is the least used letter in the alphabet, but we still need it for cool words like "quiz," "quilt," and "quick."

ACTIVITY CORNER 2

Activity 1: Multiple-Choice Quiz

Choose the correct meaning for the bold word in each sentence:

1) The **ominous** clouds warned of a terrible storm.

- a) Cheerful
- b) Threatening
- c) Bright
- d) Calm

2) She was **elated** after winning the science fair.

- a) Sad
- b) Angry
- c) Very happy
- d) Nervous

3) The student was **diligent** in completing all assignments.

- a) Lazy
- b) Hardworking
- c) Confused
- d) Carefree

Activity 2: Match the Following

Match each prefix or suffix with its correct meaning:

Prefix/Suffix	Meaning
1. Pre-	a) Full of
2. Un-	b) Before
3. -ful	c) Not
4. -less	d) Without

23

 ACTIVITY CORNER 2

Activity 3: True or False

Decide whether each statement is true or false:

1) The word "ambitious" means having a strong desire to succeed.
   a) True
   b) False

2) The prefix "re-" means to do something again.
   a) True
   b) False

3) The suffix "-ment" means full of joy.
   a) True
   b) False

Activity 4: Vocabulary Challenge – Match the Word with Its Definition

Match each vocabulary word to its correct definition:

Word	Definition
1. Precise	a) Unable to be avoided
2. Inevitable	b) Very small particle
3. Molecule	c) Exact
4. Revolution	d) Sudden and major change

3. Mastering Spelling Rules

Mastering spelling rules can be akin to cracking a code. It becomes much easier when you know the patterns. Let's explore some essential rules and fun ways to ensure that tricky words don't trip you up.

Essential Spelling Rules :

1. "I before E, except after C"

One of the oldest spelling tricks in the book! But, like all rules, it has its exceptions.

Examples:
- *Believe, Chief (I before E)*
- *Receive, Ceiling (after C)*

Exception Trivia: Did you know the word "weird" is an exception to this rule?

2. Adding -ed or -ing to a Word

When a word ends with a consonant + vowel + consonant (like "hop"), you double the last consonant before adding -ed or -ing.

Examples:
- *Hop → Hopped, Hopping*
- *Stop → Stopped, Stopping*

But if the word ends in a vowel + consonant (like "play"), just add -ed or -ing without doubling.

Example: Play → Played, Playing

3. Plurals Made Simple

- For most words, just add -s.
    - Dog → Dogs
- For words ending in ch, sh, s, x, or z, add -es.
    - Box → Boxes
    - Bus → Buses

Understanding Vowel and Consonant Patterns

Knowing how vowels and consonants work together can help you figure out the spelling of tricky words. Let's break them down!

Vowel-Consonant-Vowel (VCV) Pattern

- In these words, the vowel is usually long.
- *Example: Silent, Basic*

Consonant-Vowel-Consonant (CVC) Pattern

- In these words, the vowel is short.
- *Example: Cat, Dog*

Vowel Patterns Examples

Pattern	Word	Explanation
VCV	Silent	The vowel "i" is long.
CVC	Dog	The vowel "o" is short.
VVC	Moon	Double vowel, long "oo" sound.

Bonus Example: *"I will cite my sources" (VCV) vs. "I will sit here" (CVC).*

Common Spelling Challenges

Words with Silent Letters

- Sometimes letters decide to stay quiet!

Examples*: Knight, Write*

The "k" in "knight" and the "w" in "write" are silent but essential for spelling.

Fun Fact: The silent "k" in "knight" comes from Old English, which is how people pronounce it!

Homophones: Words That Sound Alike

Homophones are tricky because they sound the same but have different meanings and spellings.

Examples:
- *Their (possessive: "Their book")*
- *There (a place: "Over there")*
- *They're (contraction: "They are")*

Tip: Use mnemonic devices. For "their," remember that it has an "i" in it, just like "mine."

Managing Double Letters and Silent Letters

Some words seem to love double or silent letters. Here are some common ones:

- *Double Letters: Committee, Address*
   - *Example: The word "commit" has double "t."*
- *Silent Letters: Knight, Doubt*
   - *Example: The word "doubt" has a silent "b."*

Common Silent Letters

Word	Silent Letter
Knight	k
Write	w
Doubt	b

Breaking Down Compound Words

Compound words are made by joining two smaller words to form a new word. Understanding them helps with spelling and meaning.

Types of Compound Words:

- **Closed Compound Words:** Written without spaces.
    - *Example: Basketball, Homework*
- **Hyphenated Compound Words:** Connected with a hyphen.
    - *Example: Mother-in-law, Six-pack*
- **Open Compound Words:** Written as two words but function as one.
    - *Example: High school, Post office*

Spelling Rule	Explanation	Example
I before E, except after C	In most words, "i" comes before "e," unless it follows a "c."	Believe, Receive
Doubling the Final Consonant	When a word ends in consonant-vowel-consonant (CVC), double the final consonant before adding -ed or -ing.	Hop → Hopped
Adding -ed or -ing without Doubling	If a word ends in vowel-consonant (like "play"), simply add -ed or -ing without doubling the consonant.	Play → Played
Plural Rule for Most Words	Add -s to make a word plural.	Dog → Dogs
Plural Rule for Words Ending in ch, sh, s, x, z	Add -es to words ending in these letters to make them plural.	Box → Boxes, Bus → Buses
Changing -y to -ies for Plurals	If a word ends in -y preceded by a consonant, change the -y to -ies.	Baby → Babies
Silent Letters	Some letters remain silent, often due to historical origins.	Knight (silent "k")
Homophones	Words that sound the same but have different meanings and spellings.	Their, There, They're
Words Ending in -e Before Adding -ing	Drop the final -e before adding -ing to a word.	Make → Making
Words Ending in -e Before Adding -ed	Keep the -e when adding -ed.	Hope → Hoped
Changing -f to -ves for Plurals	For some words ending in -f or -fe, change the ending to -ves.	Wolf → Wolves
Using Hyphens in Compound Words	Some compound words use hyphens to join them together.	Mother-in-law
Changing Words Ending in -y to -ier/-iest	To form comparatives or superlatives of words ending in -y, change the -y to -ier or -iest.	Happy → Happier → Happiest
Dropping the Silent E for -able or -ible	Drop the -e before adding -able or -ible.	Adore → Adorable

Trivia Corner

- **The Longest Word**: The longest word in the English dictionary is pneumonoultramicroscopicsilicovolcanoconiosis, a lung disease caused by inhaling fine silica dust.

- **Weird but True:** The word "bookkeeper" (and its plural "bookkeepers") is one of the only words in English that has three consecutive double letters (oo, kk, ee).

- **"I Before E" Rule Exceptions**: The "I before E except after C" rule has more than 900 exceptions, including words like weird, height, and neither!

- **Silent Letters Surprise**: Did you know that 40% of English words have at least one silent letter? Common silent letters include k in "knight" and w in "write."

- **The Most Common Letter**: The letter E is the most frequently used letter in the English language. It appears in 11% of all words!

- **The Tricky "ough"**: The letter combination ough can be pronounced in 8 different ways! For example, thought, thought, cough, and through.

- **Words Without Vowels**: Words like rhythm and myth are examples of words without traditional vowels (a, e, i, o, u) but still have vowel sounds!

- **The Shortest Complete Sentence**: The word "I am" is the shortest sentence in English. It has both a subject and a verb.

- **Silent Letters from History**: Many silent letters exist because of old English, where people used to pronounce them. For example, people used to say "knight" as "ka-nig-hut".

- **The Most Misspelled Word**: The word "separate" is often misspelled because people mix up the "a" and "e" in the middle. Remember, it's sep-A-rate!

🎯 ACTIVITY CORNER 3

Activity 1: True or False - Spelling Rules

Read the statements below and decide if they are true or false.

1. The word "receive" follows the "I before E except after C" rule.
2. The plural of "box" is "boxs."
3. In the word "running," the last consonant is doubled because it follows the consonant-vowel-consonant pattern.
4. "Knight" and "write" both contain silent letters.
5. The word "chief" is an exception to the "I before E except after C" rule.

Activity 2: Match the Following - Silent Letters

Match each word on the left to its silent letter on the right.

Word	Silent Letter
Knight	T
Write	H
Doubt	B
Hour	W
Castle	K

Activity 3: Multiple Choice - Common Spelling Challenges

Choose the correct spelling for each word below:

1. Which is the correct spelling?
- a) Seperate
- b) Separate
- c) Seperete

 ACTIVITY CORNER 3

Activity 3: Multiple Choice - Common Spelling Challenges

Choose the correct spelling for each word below:

2. Which is the correct plural form of "bus"?
- a) Buss
- b) Busess
- c) Buses

3. Which word has the correct vowel pattern?
- a) Defanitely
- b) Definetely
- c) Definitely

Activity 4: Fix the Mistakes

Each of the sentences below contains a spelling mistake. Find and correct the mistake.

1. The nieghbor brought over some cookies.
2. I have a lot of bussiness to take care of today.
3. The rythm of the music was fast-paced.

4. Vocabulary in Everyday Life

Vocabulary in Everyday Life

What is Vocabulary?

Vocabulary is the collection of words that you know, use, and understand. The more words you know, the better you can communicate, express yourself, and comprehend what others are saying. Whether you're texting a friend, writing an essay, or chatting with family, vocabulary is essential for clear and effective communication.

How Can You Use Vocabulary in Everyday Life?

You might not even realize how often you use your vocabulary! Let's look at the ways it helps:

1) Reading: The more you read, the more new words you'll encounter. Each time you read, your vocabulary expands.

Example: R*eading a fantasy novel, you might come across the word "bewildered." This word means confused or puzzled. Now you've learned a new word!*

2) Writing: Using a wide range of words can make your writing more interesting and expressive.

Example: Instead of writing, "I was sad after losing the game," try saying: "I was devastated after losing the game." This makes your sentence more descriptive and shows a deeper emotion.

3) Speaking: When you use a variety of words in conversation, you can express yourself more clearly and even impress your friends!

Example: Instead of saying, "The pizza was good," try saying: "The pizza was delicious!" This shows you're not just satisfied—you really enjoyed it!

Applying Vocabulary in Everyday Context

Analyzing words by breaking them down into their roots, prefixes, and suffixes helps understand their meanings. For example, recognizing that "bio-" signifies life and "-logy" denotes the study of can help one comprehend that "biology" refers to the study of life.

Examples:

Instead of saying "I'm happy about the trip," you can say:

"I'm thrilled about the trip."

The word "thrilled" shows you're more than just happy—you're super excited! Choosing the right word can make a big difference in how your message comes across.

Exercise 1: Match the Everyday Phrase with a More Descriptive Word

Example Phrase:

"It's really **cold**."

Choose the better word:

- a) Freezing
- b) Chilly
- c) Scorching

Now, try these:

"I'm really tired."

- a) Exhausted
- b) Sleepy
- c) Energized

"The movie was really fun."
- a) Exciting
- b) Thrilling
- c) Boring

"I don't like this food."
- a) Dislike
- b) Hate
- c) Love

Synonyms, Antonyms, and Homophones

Vocabulary can be a lot more fun when you start exploring synonyms, antonyms, and homonyms. Let's break them down:

- **Synonyms**: Words with similar meanings.
- **Antonyms**: Words with opposite meanings.
- **Homonyms**: Words that sound the same but have different meanings.

Synonyms and Antonyms Table

Word	Synonyms	Antonyms
Happy	Joyful, Glad, Elated	Sad, Sorrowful, Miserable
Fast	Quick, Rapid, Speedy	Slow, Sluggish, Leisurely
Big	Large, Huge, Massive	Small, Tiny, Miniature
Angry	Furious, Enraged, Indignant	Calm, Peaceful, Composed
Bright	Shiny, Radiant, Luminous	Dark, Dull, Dim
Brave	Courageous, Fearless, Bold	Cowardly, Fearful, Timid
Clean	Neat, Tidy, Spotless	Dirty, Messy, Filthy
Strong	Powerful, Mighty, Sturdy	Weak, Fragile, Feeble
Hard	Tough, Difficult, Challenging	Easy, Simple, Effortless
Quiet	Silent, Peaceful, Serene	Loud, Noisy, Boisterous
Smart	Intelligent, Clever, Bright	Dumb, Foolish, Ignorant
Friendly	Kind, Warm, Sociable	Unfriendly, Cold, Hostile
Hot	Warm, Boiling, Scorching	Cold, Chilly, Freezing
Funny	Hilarious, Amusing, Comical	Serious, Solemn, Grave
Safe	Secure, Protected, Guarded	Dangerous, Risky, Hazardous
Expensive	Costly, Pricey, Overpriced	Cheap, Inexpensive, Affordable
Beautiful	Gorgeous, Stunning, Attractive	Ugly, Unattractive, Hideous
Tired	Exhausted, Fatigued, Weary	Energetic, Rested, Refreshed
Healthy	Fit, Strong, Robust	Sick, Unwell, Ill
Easy	Simple, Effortless, Straightforward	Difficult, Complicated, Complex

Homonyms Example:

- Bat (a flying mammal) vs. Bat (a tool used in baseball)
- Right (correct) vs. Write (to form letters)
- Hear (to listen) vs. Here (a location)

Homonym	Meaning 1	Meaning 2
Bark	The outer covering of a tree	The sound a dog makes
Bat	A flying mammal	A piece of sports equipment for hitting
Band	A musical group	A loop or strip used for binding
Right	Correct or accurate	The direction opposite of left
Fair	A public event with rides and games	Treating people equally
Bow	To bend forward as a gesture of respect	A knot tied with loops
Lead	To be in charge of something	A type of heavy metal (element)
Spring	A season of the year	A coil that returns to its original shape
Nail	A thin metal spike used in construction	The hard covering on the tips of fingers
Watch	To look at something carefully	A small timekeeping device worn on the wrist

Finding the Right Word for the Right Situation

Choosing the right word depends on:

- **The context**: Where and when will you use the word? *Example: You wouldn't say "What's up?" to your principal during a formal event, but it's okay with friends. Instead, you might say "Good afternoon" to your principal.*

- **The tone**: Is the word formal, informal, or humorous? *Example: Instead of saying "The weather is nice," you could say: "The weather is fantastic!" This sounds more exciting.*

- **The audience**: Who will be reading or hearing your words? *Example: You might use different words when talking to your teacher versus talking to a friend.*

Situation	Incorrect Word Choice	Correct Word Choice	Why It Works
Talking to your principal	What's up?	Good afternoon, Principal.	Formal and respectful tone for a higher authority.
Chatting with a friend	Good afternoon, buddy.	What's up?	Casual and informal language suited for friends.
Writing an essay	The weather is nice.	The weather is phenomenal.	Using more descriptive language to enhance writing.
Speaking at a formal event	This is cool.	This is extraordinary.	Formal tone appropriate for a professional audience.
Writing a thank-you note	Thanks a bunch!	I sincerely appreciate your help.	Polite and formal expression to show gratitude.
Asking for help from a teacher	I don't get it, can you help?	I am having difficulty understanding this concept.	Polite and respectful when addressing a teacher.
Giving a class presentation	So, like, this is really cool.	This topic is quite fascinating.	Professional tone for a more polished presentation.
Texting a friend	I cannot attend the event today.	Can't make it today, sorry!	Informal and brief for casual communication with friends.
Emailing a professor	Hey, I need help with this.	Dear Professor, I would appreciate your assistance.	Formal and polite tone when addressing an authority figure.
Talking about your favorite hobby	It's fun.	I really enjoy playing basketball; it's exhilarating!	Using more specific words to convey enthusiasm.

Trivia Corner

- The longest word in the English dictionary is **pneumonoultramicroscopicsilicovolcanoconiosis**. It's a type of lung disease caused by inhaling fine silicate or quartz dust. It's 45 letters long!

- The word "alphabet" comes from the first two letters of the Greek alphabet: alpha and beta.

- The word "silly" used to mean happy or fortunate in Old English. Over time, its meaning has changed to what we know today—foolish or goofy.

- The shortest complete sentence in the English language is "I am." It has a subject and a verb, making it grammatically correct!

- Some words have been around for thousands of years! For example, the word "honey" is one of the oldest known English words and hasn't changed much since ancient times.

- The word "bookkeeper" (and its related forms) is one of the only words in English with three consecutive double letters: oo, kk, and ee.

- The letter "e" is the most frequently used letter in the English language. It appears in about 11% of all English words.

- The word "quiz" comes from the word "quis," which means "who" in Latin. It was originally a game where players were asked questions.

- The word "dictionary" comes from the Latin word "dictionarium," which means "a book of words."

- The word "the" is the most common word in the English language. It appears more often than any other word!

ACTIVITY CORNER 4

Activity 1: Synonym Matching

Instructions: Match the words in Column A with their synonyms in Column B.

Column A	Column B
1. Happy	a) Furious
2. Big	b) Enormous
3. Angry	c) Delighted
4. Quiet	d) Silent
5. Fast	e) Quick

Activity 2 : Antonym Challenge

Instructions: Choose the correct antonym (opposite word) for each word listed.

1) Hot
a) Warm
b) Freezing
c) Lukewarm

2) Light
a) Bright
b) Dark
c) Glowing

3) Tough
a) Soft
b) Difficult
c) Hard

4) Happy
a) Elated
b) Sad
c) Excited

5) Loud
a) Noisy
b) Quiet
c) Silent

ACTIVITY CORNER 4
Activity 3: Homonym Hunt

Instructions: Choose the correct homonym for each sentence.

1. I left my bag over (there/their/they're).
2. She couldn't believe (there/their/they're) going to the concert.
3. Did you (hear/here) that noise last night?
4. We have to go (to/two/too) the store later.
5. The dog found (its/it's) bone in the backyard.

Activity 4: Fill in the Blanks (Context Clues)

Instructions: Fill in the blanks with the appropriate word from the word bank.
Word Bank: excited, gigantic, furious, whispered, sprinted

1. He was _____ when he won the race.
2. The dog ran _____ across the field.
3. She was _____ when she found out her phone was lost.
4. He _____ a secret to his friend.
5. The building was _____ compared to the others in town.

Activity 5: Vocabulary in Sentences

Instructions: Choose the best word to complete each sentence.

1. The athlete was feeling _____ after the marathon.
- a) exhausted
- b) happy
- c) joyful

2. The magician performed a _____ trick at the show.
- a) small
- b) mysterious
- c) funny

3. The soup was too _____ to eat.
- a) hot
- b) cold
- c) big

4. She spoke in a _____ voice during the presentation.
- a) loud
- b) clear
- c) silent

5. Reading for Vocabulary Growth

42

Reading Strategies for Vocabulary Growth

Reading is like opening a treasure chest of words. Each time you read, you discover new words and see how they're used in real situations, whether it's in a mystery novel, a comic book, or a science article. The best part is that these words become part of your own vocabulary, helping you become a better writer, speaker, and thinker.

How Reading Expands Your Vocabulary :

Reading is not only about enjoying a good story; it is also one of the most effective ways to expand your vocabulary. When you read a variety of books, articles, and even song lyrics, you are exposed to new words that you might not encounter in everyday conversation.

Example:
You're reading a fantasy book and come across this sentence:

"The ancient castle stood on a hill, its grandeur unmatched in the fading twilight."

You may not know the word "grandeur," but from the context, you can guess it means something big, impressive, or majestic. See how reading helps you learn new words without needing to look them up right away?

Reading Context Table:

Reading Example	New Word	Context Clue	Meaning
The room was immaculate, not a speck of dust in sight.	Immaculate	Not a speck of dust	Very clean, spotless
Her speech was eloquent, moving the audience to tears.	Eloquent	Moving the audience	Fluent, well-spoken
The creature was ominous, lurking in the shadows.	Ominous	Lurking in the shadows	Threatening, spooky
He watched in awe as the dancer performed with agility.	Agility	Performed with agility	Speed, flexibility

Choosing Books and Articles at Your Grade Level

It's crucial to choose the right books. If you read something too difficult, you might feel lost. On the other hand, if it's too easy, you will learn a few new words. Finding that sweet spot will help you enjoy reading and learning new vocabulary simultaneously.

Tip:
Look for books that challenge you a little but don't overwhelm you. If every page has five or more words you don't know, try something slightly easier.

Example of Suitable Books:

Grade Level	Book Title	Description
Grade 6	The Lightning Thief by Rick Riordan	A fun fantasy novel full of adventurous vocabulary and mythical creatures.
Grade 7	Wonder by R.J. Palacio	A heartwarming story that introduces emotional and descriptive language.
Grade 8	The Hunger Games by Suzanne Collins	A gripping dystopian novel with action-packed and challenging vocabulary.

Annotating Texts

When you read, don't just skim over unfamiliar words—annotate! This involves underlining, circling, or highlighting new words and writing their meanings in the margins. This not only helps you remember new words but also deepens your understanding of the story.

Example:

You're reading Wonder by R.J. Palacio and come across the word "plausible." You can write a note next to the word: "Plausible = Possible or likely to happen." This little act helps the meaning stick.

Annotating Table:

New Word	Sentence from Book	Annotation
Plausible	"It seemed plausible that she knew more than she let on."	"Plausible = Possible or likely"
Gracious	"He accepted the gift with a gracious smile."	"Gracious = Kind and polite"
Tedious	"The work was long and tedious, but necessary."	"Tedious = Boring, repetitive"

Highlighting and Defining New Words

While reading, make sure to highlight any new words you come across and then look them up later. Create a list of these words along with their definitions and examples of how they are used in sentences. Reviewing this list will help you remember the new words more effectively.

Pro Tip:
Create a vocabulary journal. Record words, meanings, and use them in sentences. Quiz yourself on new words weekly.

Vocabulary List Example:

New Word	Definition	Sentence Example
Abrupt	Sudden, without warning	The meeting came to an abrupt end when the power went out.
Jovial	Cheerful, happy	He was in a jovial mood during the holiday party.
Luminous	Bright, glowing	The luminous moon lit up the entire night sky.

Practice Exercises with Short Reading Passages

Now, it's your turn to practice! Below is a short passage with some underlined words. Use the context to figure out the meanings of these words.

Practice Passage:

The forest was serene, with the sound of birds chirping softly in the distance. The morning dew made the leaves glisten in the early sunlight, and the air was crisp and cool. As they walked, they could hear the rustling of animals in the bushes, making them feel more connected to nature.

Questions:

1. What does serene mean in the passage?
2. What do you think glisten means?
3. How would you define crisp in this context?
4. What does rustling mean in the passage?

Answers:
1. Serene: Calm, peaceful
2. Glisten: Shine, sparkle
3. Crisp: Fresh, cool
4. Rustling: Soft, crackling noise

Fun Facts About Words First Seen in Famous Books

Here's some fun trivia! Did you know that some words we use today were first seen in famous books? Check out these examples:

Word	Book	Author	Meaning
Cyberspace	Neuromancer	William Gibson	The virtual world of computers and the internet.
Muggle	Harry Potter and the Sorcerer's Stone	J.K. Rowling	A non-magical person.
Chortle	Through the Looking-Glass	Lewis Carroll	A combination of "chuckle" and "snort."
Nerd	If I Ran the Zoo	Dr. Seuss	A socially awkward person who is very focused on academics.

Create a Reading Vocabulary Journal

Now that you know how reading can supercharge your vocabulary, it's time to put it into action! Keep a Vocabulary Journal to track the new words you find while reading books, articles, or even watching movies.

How to Create Your Vocabulary Journal:
1. Pick a book or article to read.
2. Write down any new words you encounter.
3. Look up their definitions and write them down.
4. Use the word in a sentence of your own to make sure you understand it.
5. Review your words at the end of each week.

Sample Journal Entry:

Word	Book/Source	Definition	Sentence
Intricate	Harry Potter and the Goblet of Fire	Very detailed, complex	The intricate design on the cup was mesmerizing.
Perplexed	The Maze Runner	Confused, puzzled	She was perplexed by the confusing directions.
Gratitude	Wonder	Thankfulness	He expressed his gratitude for the kind gesture.

By reading regularly, annotating texts, and creating a vocabulary journal, you'll not only improve your vocabulary but also become a more confident reader and writer. Keep reading, keep learning, and soon, new words will become second nature to you!

Table : Context Clues in Reading

Reading Example	New Word	Context Clue	Meaning
The day was dreary, with gray skies and rain.	Dreary	Gray skies and rain	Gloomy, dull
He was so exhausted he could barely walk.	Exhausted	Could barely walk	Extremely tired
The view was breathtaking, with mountains as far as the eye could see.	Breathtaking	Mountains as far as the eye could see	Astonishing, stunning
She felt a sense of elation after winning the race.	Elation	After winning the race	Great happiness
The puppy was mischievous, always getting into trouble.	Mischievous	Always getting into trouble	Playfully naughty
The room was cluttered with papers and books everywhere.	Cluttered	Papers and books everywhere	Messy, disorganized
He was frantic when he couldn't find his phone.	Frantic	Couldn't find his phone	Panicked, very worried
Her dress was made of delicate lace that could tear easily.	Delicate	Could tear easily	Fragile, easily damaged
The class was attentive, listening closely to the teacher.	Attentive	Listening closely	Focused, paying attention
The landscape was desolate, with no signs of life.	Desolate	No signs of life	Empty, barren

Table : Defining New Words with Example Sentences

New Word	Definition	Example Sentence
Abrupt	Sudden, unexpected	"The fire alarm caused an abrupt end to the meeting."
Optimistic	Hopeful about the future	"She remained optimistic, even when things were tough."
Skeptical	Doubting, questioning	"He was skeptical about the new product's claims."
Gregarious	Sociable, enjoys being with others	"She was gregarious, always surrounded by friends."
Hasty	Quick and careless	"In his hasty attempt, he forgot his keys."
Luminous	Bright, glowing	"The luminous stars lit up the night sky."
Ponder	To think carefully about	"He sat in silence to ponder the meaning of the poem."
Exuberant	Filled with energy and excitement	"The children were exuberant during the birthday party."
Tedious	Boring, repetitive	"Filing papers was a tedious task, but necessary."
Inevitable	Unavoidable, certain to happen	"It was inevitable that the storm would cause delays."

Table : Challenging Vocabulary from Books

Grade Level	Book Title	New Word	Meaning	Sentence
Grade 6	The Lightning Thief by Rick Riordan	Immortal	Living forever	"The gods are immortal and cannot die."
Grade 6	Harry Potter by J.K. Rowling	Bewildered	Confused	"Harry was bewildered by the strange creatures."
Grade 7	Wonder by R.J. Palacio	Empathy	Understanding others' feelings	"He showed great empathy toward his friend."
Grade 7	Percy Jackson by Rick Riordan	Peril	Serious danger	"The heroes were in great peril during their quest."
Grade 8	The Hunger Games by Suzanne Collins	Dystopia	Imaginary world with suffering	"The Hunger Games is set in a dystopian world."
Grade 8	Divergent by Veronica Roth	Defy	Resist or challenge authority	"She was determined to defy the rules."
Grade 6	Percy Jackson by Rick Riordan	Hasty	Quick and careless	"His hasty decision led to trouble."
Grade 7	Wonder by R.J. Palacio	Obstacle	Something that blocks the way	"He overcame every obstacle in his path."
Grade 8	The Maze Runner by James Dashner	Intricate	Very detailed or complex	"The intricate maze was nearly impossible to solve."
Grade 8	The Giver by Lois Lowry	Utopia	Perfect world	"The community seemed like a utopia at first."

Table : Annotating Vocabulary in Context

New Word	Sentence from Book	Annotation
Plausible	"It seemed plausible that they would arrive soon."	Plausible = Possible, likely
Ambitious	"She had an ambitious plan to climb the tallest mountain."	Ambitious = Having a strong desire to succeed
Frugal	"He was frugal, never spending more than he needed."	Frugal = Thrifty, saving money
Compassionate	"She was compassionate and always helped others."	Compassionate = Caring, kind
Diligent	"The diligent student finished her homework early."	Diligent = Hardworking, persistent
Peculiar	"There was a peculiar noise coming from the attic."	Peculiar = Strange, odd
Gleaming	"The stars were gleaming in the night sky."	Gleaming = Shining, bright
Vivid	"The vivid colors of the painting caught my eye."	Vivid = Bright, clear
Reluctant	"He was reluctant to try the new food."	Reluctant = Hesitant, unwilling
Serene	"The lake was serene, with no disturbances."	Serene = Calm, peaceful

Table : Practice Exercise with Context Clues

Practice Passage Sentence	New Word	Context Clue	Meaning
The artist's work was intricate, with tiny, precise details.	Intricate	Tiny, precise details	Very detailed, complex
Her voice was melodious, like a beautiful song.	Melodious	Like a beautiful song	Pleasant to hear, musical
The room was dim, with only a single candle lighting it.	Dim	Single candle lighting it	Not bright
The dog was loyal, always staying by his owner's side.	Loyal	Always staying by his owner's side	Faithful, dedicated
She was clumsy, knocking over things all the time.	Clumsy	Knocking over things all the time	Awkward, uncoordinated
The atmosphere at the party was jovial, filled with laughter.	Jovial	Filled with laughter	Cheerful, happy
His explanation was vague, leaving many confused.	Vague	Leaving many confused	Unclear, not specific
The room was filled with immense tension before the test results.	Immense	Filled with tension	Huge, enormous
The cat was agile, leaping from one ledge to another.	Agile	Leaping from one ledge to another	Quick and graceful
The path was treacherous, with rocks and slippery mud.	Treacherous	Rocks and slippery mud	Dangerous, risky

Trivia Corner

The Origin of "Nerd"
- The word "nerd" was first used by Dr. Seuss in his book If I Ran the Zoo (1950).

The Longest English Word
- The longest English word in a major dictionary is "pneumonoultramicroscopicsilicovolcanoconiosis," a lung disease caused by inhaling very fine silica particles.

The Creator of "Cyberspace"
- "Cyberspace" was first coined by science fiction author William Gibson in his 1982 novel Neuromancer.

Shakespeare's Wordsmithing
- Shakespeare invented over 1,700 words, including "eyeball," "swagger," and "bedroom." His creativity helped expand the English vocabulary!

The Birth of "Quiz"
- The word "quiz" was allegedly invented in 1791 by a Dublin theater owner who bet that he could introduce a new word into the English language within 48 hours.

The Meaning of "Muggle"
- J.K. Rowling coined the word "Muggle" in the Harry Potter series to refer to non-magical people. It's now used in everyday conversation!

The Blend of "Chortle"
- "Chortle" is a combination of "chuckle" and "snort," invented by Lewis Carroll in Through the Looking-Glass (1871).

The Paradox of "Oxymoron"
- The word "oxymoron" comes from Greek words meaning "sharp" (oxy) and "foolish" (moron), which is itself an oxymoron!

The Japanese Origin of "Emoji"
- "Emoji" comes from Japanese words meaning "picture" (e) and "character" (moji), but it's often confused with the English word "emotion."

The Sandwich Story
- The word "sandwich" is named after John Montagu, the 4th Earl of Sandwich, who supposedly invented the meal so he could eat while playing cards.

ACTIVITY CORNER 5

Activity 1: Context Clues Challenge

Read the following sentences and use context clues to figure out the meaning of the underlined words.

1. The cat was so **agile** that it jumped from one tree to another with ease.
2. The movie was so **captivating** that no one looked away from the screen for the entire two hours.
3. The weather forecast predicted a **drastic** drop in temperature overnight.
4. She gave an **exemplary** performance, earning a standing ovation from the audience.
5. The cake had an **intricate** design with delicate patterns on every layer.

Activity 2 : Match the Synonym

Match the word in the left column with its synonym from the right column.

Word	Synonym
Jovial	A. Spooky
Ominous	B. Kind
Gracious	C. Cheerful
Tedious	D. Threatening
Abrupt	E. Sudden

Activity 3 : Word Detective

Read the paragraph below and identify 5 new or difficult words. Write down their meanings using the context of the passage.

Paragraph:

The **luminous** moon shone brightly in the dark sky, casting long shadows across the fields. The **serene** night was perfect for stargazing, with a gentle breeze and the faint sound of **rustling** leaves in the distance. As we sat by the fire, enjoying the **aromatic** scent of pine, we felt a sense of peace and **tranquility** that only nature can provide.

Activity 4: Fill in the Blank

Fill in the blanks with the correct word from the word bank below.

Word Bank:
- Majestic
- Plausible
- Immaculate
- Captivating
- Tedious

1. The garden was so ___ that there wasn't a single weed in sight.
2. It seemed ___ that the dog had chewed up the homework again.
3. The ___ mountains towered over the valley, casting long shadows.
4. The novel was so ___ that I read it in one sitting.
5. The job was long and ___, but it had to be done.

Activity 5: Create a Sentence

Choose five of the following words and use them in your own sentences:
- Ominous
- Luminous
- Jovial
- Serene
- Abrupt
- Plausible
- Immaculate
- Captivating

6. Word Roots, Prefixes, and Suffixes

Introduction to Roots, Prefixes, and Suffixes :

Words are like puzzles: roots, prefixes, and suffixes are the pieces that fit together to form complete words—learning how these elements work can unlock the meaning of new and unfamiliar words.

Visual: Imagine a puzzle piece with three sections—root, prefix, and suffix—fitting together.

Example:

- Root: play
- Prefix: re- + play = replay (to play again)
- Suffix: play + -er = player (a person who plays)

Latin and Greek Roots Common in Middle School Words

Many words used every day have Latin and Greek roots. Understanding these roots helps discover meanings of other words. Here are common roots and examples of words built from them:

Root	Origin	Meaning	Example Words
aqua	Latin	water	aquarium, aquatic
bio	Greek	life	biology, biography
dict	Latin	say, speak	dictionary, predict
geo	Greek	earth	geography, geology
tele	Greek	far	telephone, telescope
therm	Greek	heat	thermometer, thermal
port	Latin	carry	transport, portable

Expanding Vocabulary with Affixes

Prefixes and suffixes are like accessories you can add to a root word to change its meaning or even its part of speech. This helps you expand your vocabulary in a snap!

Table of Common Affixes:

Prefix	Meaning	Example Word	Suffix	Meaning	Example Word
un-	not	unhappy = not happy	-ful	full of	joyful = full of joy
re-	again	rewrite = write again	-less	without	hopeless = without hope
pre-	before	preview = see before	-ly	how something is done	quickly = done quickly

Activity: Fill in the blanks by adding prefixes or suffixes to the root words below:

1. Root: play + re- = _____
2. Root: hope + -less = _____
3. Root: write + re- = _____
4. Root: quick + -ly = _____

Answers:

1. Replay
2. Hopeless
3. Rewrite
4. Quickly

How Latin and Greek Roots Shape Everyday English

- Did you know? The word "telephone" comes from the Greek roots tele (far) and phone (sound), meaning "far sound."
- Aquarium comes from the Latin root aqua, meaning water.
- Scientific terms like biology (study of life) and geology (study of Earth) use Greek roots!
- The prefix re- is commonly used in words like "redo" (to do again) and "recycle" (to use again).
- Words like "superhero" come from the prefix super (above) and the root hero.

Build Your Own Word Trees with Roots and Affixes

Instructions: Create your own word tree using a root word and branching out with different prefixes and suffixes.

1. Choose a root word (e.g., port).
2. Draw a tree with the root word as the trunk.
3. For each branch, add a prefix or suffix to form a new word.

Example Word Tree for Root "Port":
- Transport: to carry across
- Portable: able to be carried
- Import: to bring in from another place

Root Word	Meaning	Example Words	Definitions
Bio	Life (Greek)	Biology, Biography, Biome, Biologist, Biosphere	Biology: Study of life; Biography: Written account of someone's life
Aqua	Water (Latin)	Aquarium, Aquatic, Aquifer, Aquaplane, Aquamarine	Aquarium: A tank for aquatic animals; Aquatic: Relating to water
Chron	Time (Greek)	Chronicle, Chronology, Chronometer, Synchronize, Chronic	Chronicle: Historical account; Synchronize: To occur at the same time

Dict	Speak (Latin)	Dictate, Dictionary, Prediction, Contradict, Dictator	Dictionary: Book of words; Predict: Say what will happen in the future
Geo	Earth (Greek)	Geography, Geology, Geothermal, Geode, Geometry	Geography: Study of Earth's surface; Geometry: Math dealing with shapes
Manu	Hand (Latin)	Manual, Manufacture, Manuscript, Manipulate, Manicure	Manual: A handbook; Manufacture: To make by hand or machine
Therm	Heat (Greek)	Thermometer, Thermos, Thermal, Thermostat, Hypothermia	Thermometer: Measures temperature; Hypothermia: Dangerous body temp drop
Aud	Hear (Latin)	Audience, Audible, Audiobook, Auditorium, Audition	Audience: Group listening; Audition: Tryout to be heard
Luc	Light (Latin)	Lucid, Illuminate, Translucent, Luminous, Lucent	Lucid: Clear or easy to understand; Illuminate: To light up
Pathos	Feeling/Suffering (Greek)	Sympathy, Empathy, Pathology, Pathetic, Apathy	Sympathy: Feeling for someone; Empathy: Understanding others' feelings

Table of prefixes and suffixes

Type	Prefix/Suffix	Meaning	Example Word	Explanation
Prefix	Un-	Not, opposite of	Unhappy	Unhappy means not happy. The prefix un- changes the meaning to the opposite.
Prefix	Re-	Again	Rewrite	Rewrite means to write again. The prefix re- indicates repetition.
Prefix	Pre-	Before	Preview	Preview means to see before. The prefix pre- refers to something that happens earlier.
Prefix	Dis-	Not, opposite of	Disagree	Disagree means to not agree. The prefix dis- forms a negative meaning.
Prefix	Mis-	Wrongly	Misunderstand	Misunderstand means to understand wrongly. The prefix mis- indicates an error.
Suffix	-ful	Full of	Hopeful	Hopeful means full of hope. The suffix -ful shows that someone has hope.
Suffix	-less	Without	Fearless	Fearless means without fear. The suffix -less indicates the absence of something.
Suffix	-er	A person who does	Teacher	Teacher refers to a person who teaches. The suffix -er is used for someone who performs an action.
Suffix	-ly	In a certain way	Quickly	Quickly means in a fast way. The suffix -ly turns an adjective into an adverb.

Trivia Corner

- *Did you know? The word "biology" comes from the Greek root "bio-" meaning "life" and "-logy" meaning "study of." So, biology literally means "the study of life."*

- *Fun fact! The word "television" combines "tele-" (Greek for "far") and "-vision" (Latin for "seeing"). It means "seeing from a distance."*

- *Origin alert! The word "astronaut" is made up of two Greek roots: "astro-" meaning "star" and "-naut" meaning "sailor." An astronaut is essentially a "star sailor."*

- *Bet you didn't know! The prefix "mega-" comes from Greek, meaning "large" or "great." That's why we call something enormous a "megastore" or "megacity."*

- *Surprise fact! The suffix "-phobia" comes from Greek, meaning "fear." Words like "arachnophobia" (fear of spiders) and "claustrophobia" (fear of confined spaces) all share this suffix.*

- *Word mash-up! The word "autograph" is a combination of "auto-" (Greek for "self") and "-graph" (Greek for "write"). It literally means "self-writing," which is why it refers to your signature.*

- *Language mix! The word "automobile" combines a Greek prefix "auto-" (self) and a Latin root "mobilis" (movable). Together, it means "self-movable" — which makes sense for a car!*

- *Rooted in history! The Latin word "dict-" means "say" or "speak." That's why words like "dictate," "dictionary," and "predict" all have something to do with speaking or saying.*

- *Hidden science! The word "photosynthesis" is formed from Greek roots: "photo-" meaning "light" and "-synthesis" meaning "putting together." It refers to plants using light to create food.*

- *Did you know? The suffix "-ology" means "the study of." So, words like "psychology" (study of the mind) and "geology" (study of the earth) share this common ending.*

 ACTIVITY CORNER 6

Activity 1: Word Roots Puzzle

Fill in the puzzle using the provided clues related to word roots and affixes.

Clues:
1. Greek root meaning "light"
2. Latin root meaning "to write"
3. Prefix meaning "self"
4. Suffix meaning "study of"
5. Prefix meaning "before"

Activity 2: Match the Prefix and Meaning

Match the prefix with its correct meaning.

Prefix	Meaning
1. Anti-	A. After
2. Sub-	B. Against
3. Hyper-	C. Again
4. Post-	D. Under
5. Re-	E. Over, excessive

Activity 3 : Create Words from Roots

Using the roots below, form new words by adding prefixes or suffixes.

Root Word	Prefix/Suffix	New Word
Spect	-acle	_____
Dict	Pre-	_____
Form	Re-	_____
Port	Ex-	_____
Act	-ion	_____

Activity 4: Identify the Root and its Meaning

Below are words that contain Latin or Greek roots. Identify the root in each word and explain its meaning. Write your answers in the blanks provided.

1) Biology
- Root: _____
- Meaning: _____

2) Transport
- Root: _____
- Meaning: _____

3) Autograph
- Root: _____
- Meaning: _____

4) Predict
- Root: _____
- Meaning: _____

5) Photograph
- Root: _____
- Meaning: _____

6) Television
- Root: _____
- Meaning: _____

7) Construct
- Root: _____
- Meaning: _____

8) Thermometer
- Root: _____
- Meaning: _____

9) Hydrate
- Root: _____
- Meaning: _____

10) Manual
- Root: _____
- Meaning: _____

7. Spelling with Confidence : A Fun and Challenging Adventure

Tackling Tricky Words: A Spelling Safari

Have you ever encountered a word that doesn't seem to follow the rules? These sneaky words, often referred to as "tricky words," can be quite puzzling. They may have silent letters, unexpected vowel sounds, or unusual letter combinations. Let's go on a spelling safari to conquer these tricky words!

Type of Tricky Word	Example Word	Common Mistake	Spelling Tip
Silent Letters	Know	Now	Remember: The "k" is silent but still there!
Unexpected Vowel Sounds	Laugh	Laguh	The "a" sounds like "ah," not "ay"
Unusual Letter Combinations	Friend	Frend	Think of a "friend" and not a "fiend"
Silent Letters	Knight	Nite	The "k" is silent, but a knight fights with honor!

Multisyllabic Mastery: Breaking Down Words

Big words can be intimidating, but they're easier to handle when you break them down into smaller parts called syllables. Think of it like breaking up a giant pizza into slices—it's easier to eat!

Word	Syllables	How to Break It Down
Opportunity	op-por-tu-ni-ty	Say it slow: "op-POR-tu-ni-ty"
Ambition	am-bi-tion	Say it slow: "am-BI-tion"
Education	ed-u-ca-tion	Say it slow: "ed-U-ca-tion"
Communication	com-mu-ni-ca-tion	Say it slow: "com-MU-ni-ca-tion"

Homophone Heroes: Choosing the Right Word

Some words sound the same but have different meanings and spellings. These are called homophones; picking the right one is vital to clear writing!

Homophones	Meaning	Example Sentence
Their	Belonging to them	They forgot their books at school.
There	Refers to a place	Put your bag over there.
They're	Short for they are	They're going to the party.
Your	Belonging to you	Is that your pencil?
You're	Short for you are	You're going to ace the spelling test!

Memory Magic: Mnemonics and Visualization

Mnemonics and visualization are powerful tools for remembering tricky spellings. Mnemonics are short phrases or tricks, while visualization involves creating mental images to remember a word's spelling.

Examples: Common Mnemonics

- Because: **B**ig **E**lephants **C**an **A**lways **U**nderstand **S**mall **E**lephants
- Rhythm: **R**hythm **H**elps **Y**our **T**wo **H**ips **M**ove

Word	Mnemonic
Ne**cess**ary	One **C**ollar and Two **S**leeves are Necessary
Sepa**rat**e	There is a rat in separate

50 Commonly Misspelled Words and Tricks to Remember Them

Word	Trick to Remember
Accommodate	Remember: It has two c's and two m's. Think of "a comfy room" that accommodates.
Definitely	It has "finite" inside it, not "definately." Think: "It's definite, not infinite."
Separate	Think of the rat in the middle: separate.
Receive	Remember the "I before E except after C" rule: receive.
Necessary	One collar (c) and two sleeves (s). Neck and sleeves help you remember the spelling.
Embarrass	This word has two r's and two s's—"You wouldn't want to bare too much!"
Friend	A friend will always be at the end of your worries, so it ends with "end".
Calendar	Remember, "ar" at the end, like "A calendar has all your dates."
Argument	Drop the e after argue, making it argument.
Business	Think of the word busy first: "Busy people do business."
Beginning	It begins with "beg" and has two n's in the middle.
Tomorrow	It has one m and two r's. You "borrow" an "r" from tomorrow!
Weird	Exception to the rule! "We are a weird bunch."
Restaurant	Remember: rest-au-rant (pronounce each part clearly in your head).
Privilege	The word has "lege" at the end. Think of the privilege of legal rights.
Occasion	There are two c's but only one s. You need a special occasion to spell it right.
Definitely	"Definite" has finite inside it. It's not infinite, it's finite!
Separate	Remember, there's a rat in the middle: separat**e.
Sincerely	Think: A sincere person never lies, and never skips the e after the c.
Disappoint	It has one s and two p's. You never want to double disappoint someone.
Maintenance	Think of it as maintain with an "ance" at the end.

50 Commonly Misspelled Words and Tricks to Remember Them

Word	Trick to Remember
Beautiful	Remember B-E-A-Utiful! Say it out loud like Jim Carrey in Bruce Almighty.
Recommend	Think of giving a commendation. Double the c and m.
Separate	Again, don't forget the rat in separate!
Believe	"I believe" follows "I before E except after C."
Success	Success has double c's and double s's. Double your chances for success!
Guarantee	I guarantee the letter 'a' is always in the right place.
Misspell	Ironically, misspell is often misspelled. It has two s's!
Fulfill	You are "full" of "fulfillment". It's one l in the middle, two at the end.
Occurred	It has two c's and two r's. Think of a double occurrence of letters.
Absence	Remember, there's a silent s in ab-sense!
Government	It has an n in the middle, like "govern-ment."
Conscience	Con and science together. Be mindful like a scientist!
Humorous	Think of being humorous like a clown—no "u" after the "o."
Environment	Break it into en-viron-ment to make it easier to remember.
Occurred	Think of the r occurring twice.
Knowledge	There is a silent k at the beginning, like in "knock."
Noticeable	It's notice plus able. Don't forget the e after "c"!
Hierarchy	It has hier at the start, like in "higher up."
Intelligence	Intel is smart—don't forget the g.
License	"Can I have my license to drive?" (Sounds like "lice").
Acknowledgment	Don't forget the e after "g" like in "knowledge"!
Appearance	Remember: appear + ance.
Criticize	Even critics follow the rule: c comes first, then z!
Neighbor	A neighbor is someone who lives "nearby" (ei).
Curiosity	Think of a curious cat!
Unnecessary	Think: Double "n" because it's not necessary twice!
Restaurant	A rest-au-rant serves food.
Occurrence	Two c's and two r's make it a double occurrence.
Experience	Think of the "ex" at the start like exciting experiences.
Rhythm	Rhy-thm (no vowels but pronounced rhythmically).
Grateful	Remember: You are grateful because of great things.
Visible	The ible ending shows it is visible to your eyes!
Possession	It's possess plus ion. Double the s's to own it!

Trivia Corner

The Shortest Sentence:
- "I am." This tiny sentence packs a big punch! It's the shortest complete sentence in English, showing how even a few words can convey a thought.

The Word "Rhythm" Has No Vowels:
- Rhythm is a unique word because it doesn't contain any traditional vowels (a, e, i, o, u). The letter "y" takes on the vowel sound.

"Q" Always Needs a "U":
- Q is almost always followed by the letter "u." Can you think of any words that break this rule? There are a few exceptions, like "Qatar" and "qanat."

"I Before E Except After C" Has Exceptions:
- While the famous spelling rule is helpful, there are exceptions. Words like "weird," "seize," and "science" don't follow the pattern.

The Word "Queue" Is All About the First Letter:
- Queue is a fascinating word because if you remove the last four letters ("ueue"), you still have the same pronunciation.

Silent Letters Were Once Pronounced:
- Words like "knight" and "gnat" used to have their silent letters pronounced. Over time, the pronunciation changed, but the spelling remained the same.

Longest One-Syllable Words:
- Screeched is the longest one-syllable word in English, with its double letters and unusual combination.

"Mississippi" Is a Spelling Champ:
- Mississippi is a popular word for students to learn because of its repetitive pattern.

The Word "Floccinaucinihilipilification":
- This long word means "the act of estimating something as worthless." It's a fun challenge for spelling enthusiasts!

"W" in "Two" Is Silent but Important:
Even though the "w" in "two" is silent, it's crucial for distinguishing it from "to" and "too." Silent letters play a role in word meaning and pronunciation.

ACTIVITY CORNER 7

Activity 1: Unscramble the Words
Instructions: Unscramble the letters to find the correct word.

1. nticidfeely
2. rscocrrue
3. tarmuosre
4. cmoedremn
5. gmmirforap

Activity 2: Multiple Choice - Choose the Correct Homophone
Instructions: Choose the correct homophone for each sentence.

1. I think (their/they're/there) going to the concert tomorrow.
2. Did you bring (your/you're) homework to class today?
3. Please put the book (over their/over there).
4. (Your/You're) an amazing speller!
5. They forgot (their/they're/there) backpacks at school.

Activity 3 : Fill-in-the-Blank Spelling
Instructions: Fill-in-the-Blank Spelling
Word Bank: excitement, recommend , disappointed, sign, necessary

1. The teacher will _____ the best book for you to read.
2. I will _____ the letter with my name at the end.
3. It is _____ to study for your spelling test.
4. She felt a lot of _____ when she saw her friends.
5. The dog was _____ that he didn't get a treat.

Activity 4 : Match the word from the left column with its correct definition from the right column.
Instructions: Fill-in-the-Blank Spelling

Word	Definition
1. Guarantee	a. A strong recommendation
2. Privilege	b. A promise that something will happen
3. Recommend	c. A special right or advantage
4. Accommodate	d. Make room or space for something
5. Intelligence	e. The ability to acquire and apply knowledge

8. Vocabulary in Writing

This chapter will help you improve your writing by expanding your vocabulary. You will learn how to transition from simple words to richer vocabulary, avoid repetitive words, and use a thesaurus effectively. The chapter includes fun tables, examples, trivia, and activities to help you become a word wizard!

Boosting Your Writing with Strong Vocabulary

Having a strong vocabulary can make your writing more impressive. While words like "nice" or "good" are sufficient, using more descriptive and precise words can make your writing more engaging. This section demonstrates how to replace simple words with stronger, more specific ones.

Simple vs. Strong Vocabulary

Simple Word	Stronger Alternative	Example Sentence with Stronger Word
Good	Excellent, Outstanding	She did an outstanding job on her project.
Big	Enormous, Gigantic	The enormous tree towered over the house.
Said	Exclaimed, Whispered	"Hurry up!" she exclaimed as they ran to catch the bus.
Happy	Joyful, Ecstatic	He felt ecstatic after winning the game.
Bad	Awful, Terrible	The weather was awful, with rain pouring all day.
Small	Tiny, Minuscule	The tiny kitten fit into the palm of my hand.
Fast	Swift, Speedy	The runner was swift, crossing the finish line in seconds.
Sad	Miserable, Gloomy	The movie was so gloomy, it made everyone cry.

Transitioning from Simple Words to Richer Vocabulary

It's easy to rely on everyday words in your writing, but stronger vocabulary adds depth. Let's look at how you can transition from simple words to richer vocabulary with the help of a thesaurus.

Example Table: Word Transition

Basic Word	Richer Vocabulary	Example Sentence
Walk	Stroll, Stride, March	She went for a stroll in the park after dinner.
Look	Glance, Gaze, Observe	He took a quick glance at his watch.
Nice	Kind, Considerate, Generous	The teacher was very kind to help us with our homework.
Run	Sprint, Dash, Scamper	The rabbit scampered across the field.
Scared	Terrified, Anxious	She was anxious before her big exam.
Tired	Exhausted, Weary	After the long hike, I was completely exhausted.

Activity:
- Think of three sentences where you used basic words like "happy" or "big." Rewrite those sentences by choosing a richer word from the table above.
- Example: Instead of "She was happy," try "She was ecstatic."

Avoiding Repetitive Words

Using the same word repeatedly can make your writing monotonous. A skilled writer uses a variety of words to keep the reader interested. This section helps you avoid repetitive words by substituting them with synonyms

Example: Before and After

- Before: The cat was happy when it got a treat. The happy cat purred.
- After: The cat was joyful when it got a treat. The ecstatic cat purred.

Exercise: Rewrite These Sentences to Avoid Repetition

Original Sentence	Improved Version
The movie was good, and the food was good too.	The movie was excellent, and the food was delicious.
It was a nice day, and we had a nice time.	It was a beautiful day, and we had a wonderful time.

Using a Thesaurus Effectively

A thesaurus is a valuable resource for finding synonyms, but it should be used carefully. Just because a word is listed as a synonym doesn't mean it will be suitable in every context. Context matters!

Example: Using a Thesaurus Correctly

Incorrect Use	Why It's Wrong
The soup was brilliant.	"Brilliant" describes intelligence or brightness, not taste.
The chair was exquisite.	"Exquisite" is too fancy for describing a basic chair.

Correct Use	Why It Works
The soup was delicious.	"Delicious" accurately describes the flavor of the soup.
The chair was comfortable.	"Comfortable" is the right word to describe a chair.

Tip: After finding a word in a thesaurus, read it in a sentence to see if it fits. Ask yourself: "Does this word make sense here?

Practice Exercises on Integrating Vocabulary in Writing

Let's practice using stronger vocabulary in your writing. For each sentence, replace the basic word with a richer vocabulary word from the word bank below.

Exercise: Rewrite These Sentences with Stronger Vocabulary

1. The boy ran quickly to the park.
2. The movie was good, and we had fun.
3. She said she would come to the party.
4. The cake was nice, and everyone liked it.
5. It was a big house, and we had a great time exploring.

Word Bank:
- Sprint, Delightful, Excellent, Exclaimed, Generous, Enormous, Enjoyed

Answers to Practice Exercises:

1. The boy sprinted to the park.
2. The movie was excellent, and we had fun.
3. She exclaimed that she would come to the party.
4. The cake was delightful, and everyone liked it.
5. It was an enormous house, and we had a great time exploring.

Example Table: Simple vs. Strong Vocabulary

Simple Word	Stronger Alternative	Example Sentence with Stronger Word
Good	Excellent, Outstanding	She did an outstanding job on her project.
Big	Enormous, Gigantic	The enormous tree towered over the house.
Said	Exclaimed, Whispered	"Hurry up!" she exclaimed as they ran to catch the bus.
Happy	Joyful, Ecstatic	He felt ecstatic after winning the game.
Bad	Awful, Terrible	The weather was awful, with rain pouring all day.

Simple Word	Stronger Alternative	Example Sentence with Stronger Word
Small	Tiny, Minuscule	The tiny kitten fit into the palm of my hand.
Fast	Swift, Speedy	The runner was swift, crossing the finish line in seconds.
Sad	Miserable, Gloomy	The movie was so gloomy, it made everyone cry.
Cold	Chilly, Freezing	The night was freezing, and we stayed by the fire.
Hot	Scorching, Sweltering	The sun was scorching during the afternoon.
Nice	Kind, Generous	The teacher was very kind to help me after class.
Fun	Exciting, Entertaining	The roller coaster ride was incredibly exciting.
Scared	Terrified, Horrified	He was terrified of the thunderstorm.
Angry	Furious, Enraged	She was furious when she heard the news.
Smart	Brilliant, Intelligent	The scientist came up with a brilliant solution.
Tired	Exhausted, Weary	After the marathon, she felt completely exhausted.
Hungry	Famished, Starving	I was famished after skipping breakfast.
Old	Ancient, Aged	The ancient ruins were fascinating to explore.
Pretty	Gorgeous, Stunning	The sunset was absolutely stunning that evening.
Hard	Difficult, Challenging	The math test was very challenging for most students.

Example Table: Word Transitions

Basic Word	Richer Vocabulary	Example Sentence
Walk	Stroll, Stride, March	We went for a stroll along the beach in the evening.
Look	Glance, Gaze, Observe	She gave a quick glance at the clock during the meeting.
Nice	Pleasant, Agreeable	We had a pleasant conversation over lunch.
Run	Sprint, Dash, Scamper	The squirrel scampered up the tree to escape.
Scared	Frightened, Alarmed	I was frightened when I heard the loud noise outside.
Tired	Fatigued, Drained	After the long hike, I was completely drained of energy.
Quiet	Silent, Tranquil	The park was tranquil, with only the sound of birds chirping.
Talk	Chat, Converse	We had a quick chat before class started.
Laugh	Giggle, Chuckle	The joke made her giggle during the movie.
Cry	Sob, Weep	He began to sob after losing his favorite toy.
Love	Adore, Cherish	She adores her puppy and takes care of it every day.
Help	Assist, Support	The teacher was always there to assist me with my homework.
Hate	Detest, Loathe	She detests waking up early for school.
Win	Triumph, Conquer	Our team triumphed in the soccer championship.
Fight	Battle, Struggle	The soldiers battled bravely for their country.
Eat	Devour, Munch	He devoured his meal after playing outside all day.
Sleep	Doze, Slumber	She fell into a deep slumber after a long day at the beach.
Jump	Leap, Bound	The kangaroo leaped across the field with ease.
Think	Reflect, Contemplate	He reflected on his choices before making a decision.
Bright	Luminous, Radiant	The stars were radiant in the clear night sky.

Example Table: Before and After

Before	After
The cat was happy when it got a treat. The happy cat purred.	The cat was joyful when it got a treat. The ecstatic cat purred.
The movie was good and the food was good too.	The movie was excellent, and the food was delicious too.
It was a nice day and we had a nice time.	It was a beautiful day and we had a wonderful time.
The teacher said we would have a test. Then, she said it would be hard.	The teacher announced we would have a test. Then, she warned it would be hard.
She was scared of the dark and scared of loud noises.	She was frightened of the dark and terrified of loud noises.
The girl was happy to win, and her friends were happy too.	The girl was thrilled to win, and her friends were overjoyed too.
He ran fast in the race, and his teammate ran fast too.	He sprinted in the race, and his teammate dashed as well.
The room was big, and the hall was big too.	The room was spacious, and the hall was enormous.
They had a good time at the party and a good meal.	They had a fantastic time at the party and a delightful meal.
It was a bad day because of the bad weather.	It was a terrible day because of the stormy weather.
The teacher was nice, and her students were nice too.	The teacher was kind, and her students were polite too.
The book was interesting, and the movie was interesting too.	The book was fascinating, and the movie was captivating too.
The dog was angry at the mailman and angry at the cat.	The dog was furious at the mailman and irritated at the cat.
The water was cold, and the air was cold too.	The water was freezing, and the air was chilly too.
The cake was nice, and the cookies were nice too.	The cake was delicious, and the cookies were scrumptious too.

Example Table: Using a Thesaurus Correctly

Incorrect Use	Why It's Wrong
The weather was amazing when it rained.	"Amazing" usually describes something impressive or surprising, not rain.
The cookies were huge in taste.	"Huge" refers to size, not taste.
The homework was delightful.	"Delightful" describes something pleasant or enjoyable, not homework.

Correct Use	Why It's Right
The sunset was breathtaking as it dipped below the horizon.	"Breathtaking" describes something beautiful or awe-inspiring, which fits a sunset.
The cookies were delicious and full of flavor.	"Delicious" accurately describes the taste of the cookies.
The homework was challenging, but I enjoyed learning.	"Challenging" appropriately describes the difficulty of homework.

Trivia Corner

- *Did you know? The average person only uses about 5,000-6,000 words in their daily conversations, but the English language contains over 170,000 words!*
- *Fun Fact: Shakespeare is credited with inventing over 1,700 words in the English language, including common ones like eyeball, bedroom, and gossip!*
- *Word Power: The word "alphabet" comes from the first two letters of the Greek alphabet: "alpha" and "beta."*
- *Synonym Surprise: The word "run" has the most definitions in the English language — it can mean over 645 different things depending on how it's used!*
- *Record-Breaker: The longest word in an English dictionary is pneumonoultramicroscopicsilicovolcanoconiosis—a type of lung disease caused by inhaling fine silica dust.*
- *Thesaurus Trivia: The first thesaurus was created by Peter Mark Roget in 1852 and was originally titled "Thesaurus of English Words and Phrases." It was designed to help people find alternative words.*
- *Vocabulary Booster: Learning just one new word each day can add up to learning 365 new words in a year!*
- *Homophone Heads-Up: The words "right," "write," "rite," and "wright" sound the same but mean completely different things. They're called homophones.*
- *Repeat Offenders: The most commonly overused word in English writing is "very." Try replacing it with a stronger adjective to make your writing more impactful!*
- *Rich Vocabulary: Studies show that people who read regularly tend to have a vocabulary that's 50% larger than those who don't read much.*
- *Origin Stories: The word "sandwich" comes from the Earl of Sandwich, who invented it so he could eat without stopping his card games.*
- *Big Impact Words: Some of the shortest words in English, like "if" and "no", can have the biggest impact in conversation and writing.*
- *Colorful Expressions: The English language has more words for "blue" than for any other color. Think of navy, cobalt, sky, royal, and more!*
- *Changing Meanings: The word "awful" used to mean "full of awe" or amazing, but over time its meaning changed to something bad.*
- *Word Evolution: The word "nice" originally meant "ignorant" in the 14th century, but today, it means kind or friendly.*

 ACTIVITY CORNER 8

Activity 1: Match the Following

Match the simple word with its richer synonym from the options below:

Simple Word	Options (Synonyms)
1. Big	a) Astonishing
2. Small	b) Massive
3. Happy	c) Tiny
4. Sad	d) Elated
5. Surprising	e) Melancholy

Activity 2: Choose the Correct Option

Pick the best vocabulary word to complete each sentence:

1. The dog was very (friendly/ferocious) to the children.
2. She completed her homework with (precision/sloppiness) and got full marks.
3. The magician's trick was (mysterious/boring) and left the audience in awe.
4. After running for an hour, I was (exhausted/energetic).
5. The storm caused (extensive/tiny) damage to the town.

Activity 3: Fill in the Blank

Use the words from the word bank to fill in the blanks:

Word Bank: fascinated, enormous, radiant, anxious, swift

1. The sun was shining so brightly, it looked _____.
2. The children were _____ to open their birthday presents.
3. The _____ mountains towered over the valley below.
4. She was _____ by the magician's amazing performance.
5. The rabbit was _____ as it hopped across the field.

ACTIVITY CORNER 8

Activity 4 : Substitute with a Better Word

Rewrite the sentences using a stronger word from the word bank to replace the underlined word::

Word Bank: exceptional, terrifying, hilarious, crucial, spectacular

1. The movie was very <u>funny.</u>
2. The rollercoaster ride was <u>very scary.</u>
3. Winning the championship was an <u>important</u> moment for the team.
4. Her performance in the play was <u>really good</u>.
5. The fireworks display on the Fourth of July was <u>very impressive.</u>

Activity 5 : Synonym Search – Find Better Words

Replace the underlined words in the sentences with richer vocabulary:

1. The cake was <u>good.</u>
2. He felt <u>bad</u> after the argument.
3. The view from the mountain was <u>beautiful.</u>
4. The book was <u>interesting</u>.
5. She was <u>mad</u> at her brother for breaking her toy.

79

9. Proofreading for Spelling and Vocabulary Errors

Introduction

Proofreading is an essential skill for writing clearly and effectively. It helps ensure that your spelling, vocabulary, and grammar are correct, making your writing easier to understand. In this chapter, we will explore techniques for spotting and fixing errors, the power of technology, and how to proofread like a pro!

Techniques for Catching Spelling Mistakes

Even the best writers make spelling mistakes, but the good news is that there are techniques to help you catch them. These methods will sharpen your eye for errors and improve your accuracy.

Tip 1: Read Backwards

- Start at the end of your writing and read each word backwards. This forces you to look at each word individually, which makes it easier to spot spelling mistakes.

Tip 2: Say Each Word Out Loud

- Sometimes, our brains skim over mistakes when we read silently. By saying each word out loud, you might catch something that looks or sounds wrong.

Tip 3: Look for Commonly Misspelled Words

- Certain words are tricky for many students. Keep an eye out for these common spelling troublemakers:
    - their/they're/there
    - your/you're
    - receive (Remember: "i before e except after c!")

Table: Commonly Misspelled Words and Tricks

Word	Trick to Remember
Definitely	Remember: "It's definitely not definately!"
Separate	Think: "There's a rat in separate."
Believe	Use the saying: "I believe in 'i before e'!"
Friend	Remember: "A friend is always there till the end."
Necessary	Think: "It's necessary to have one 'c' and two 's'."

Using Technology to Help Proofread :

Technology can be a valuable tool for proofreading, with many available resources to help you catch errors in your work.

Tip 1: Spell Check

- Most word processing software has built-in spell checkers. They can highlight misspelled words, but remember, they're not perfect. You still need to double-check!

Tip 2: Grammar Check

- Some tools, like Grammarly or Microsoft Word's grammar feature, can help you spot grammatical errors or improve your word choice. Be cautious—these tools don't catch everything.

Tip 3: Online Dictionaries and Thesauruses

- Use online dictionaries to confirm spelling and a thesaurus to find synonyms if you've used a word too many times.

Editing Your Work

Editing involves more than just correcting spelling errors. It is about ensuring that your writing is clear, flows well, and utilizes strong vocabulary.

Tip 1: Take a Break
- After finishing your writing, take a break before proofreading. This gives your brain a rest and makes it easier to spot mistakes when you return.

Tip 2: Focus on One Type of Error at a Time
- Start by reading your work once to check for spelling, then read it again to focus on vocabulary or grammar.

Tip 3: Use a Checklist
- Create a proofreading checklist. Here's a sample checklist you can use:

Proofreading Checklist

1. Check for spelling mistakes
2. Look for repeated words
3. Make sure each sentence makes sense
4. Ensure your vocabulary is rich and varied
5. Check for punctuation errors
6. Correct any subject-verb agreement mistakes

Spotting Vocabulary and Grammar Errors

Vocabulary and grammar are essential parts of writing. Strong word choices and correct grammar help convey your message clearly.

Tip 1: Look for Repeated Words

- Repetition can make your writing sound boring. Try to find synonyms or different ways to phrase your ideas.

Example:
- *Original:* "The book was very interesting because it had interesting characters and an interesting plot."
- *Improved:* "The book was fascinating because it had captivating characters and an exciting plot."

Tip 2: Be Careful with Homophones

- Homophones are words that sound the same but have different meanings. Be sure to use the correct one!

Common Homophones Table

Homophones	Meaning	Example in a Sentence
Their/There/They're	Their = belonging to them, There = location, They're = they are	Their dog is over there; they're going to pick it up.
Your/You're	Your = belonging to you, You're = you are	Your pencil is on the desk; you're going to need it for the quiz.
Its/It's	Its = belonging to it, It's = it is	The dog wagged its tail; it's a very happy dog.
To/Two/Too	To = direction, Two = number, Too = also	I am going to the park with my two friends, and they're coming too.

Common spelling and vocabulary errors :

25 common spelling and vocabulary errors frequently made by middle school students.

Common Error	Correct Version	Tip/Trick to Remember	Example Sentence (Correct Usage)
Alot	A lot	"A lot" is two words, not one.	There is a lot of homework to do this weekend.
Definately	Definitely	Think "definite" + "ly" = definitely.	I will definitely go to the party on Saturday.
Seperate	Separate	There's a "rat" in separate.	Keep your school and personal life separate.
Their/There/They're	Their, There, They're	"Their" is possession, "There" is a place, "They're" = they are.	Their house is over there, and they're coming soon.
Your/You're	Your, You're	"Your" is possession, "You're" means "you are."	You're going to need your notebook today.
Its/It's	Its, It's	"Its" is possession, "It's" means "it is."	The dog wagged its tail because it's happy.
Then/Than	Than, Then	"Than" is for comparison; "Then" refers to time.	I am taller than my brother, and then we went to play basketball.
Wich	Which	Remember: "Which" has two 'h's like a "witch on Halloween."	Which book did you borrow from the library?
Recieve	Receive	I before E, except after C.	I was happy to receive the letter from my friend.
Accomodate	Accommodate	"Accommodation" has double 'c' and 'm'.	The hotel will accommodate all guests.
Excercise	Exercise	"Exercise" has "cise" like "scissors" because you cut calories.	I exercise every morning before school.
Febuary	February	"February" has an extra 'r' after 'b'.	February is the shortest month of the year.
Tommorow	Tomorrow	"Tomorrow" has two 'r's, like racing to the future.	Tomorrow, we have a math test.
Wednsday	Wednesday	Break it down: "Wed-nes-day."	Wednesday is the middle of the school week.
Embarras	Embarrass	"Embarrass" has double 'r' and 's' – don't let them embarrass you!	I felt embarrassed when I tripped in front of the class.
Begining	Beginning	Remember: Two 'n's in the middle.	The beginning of the story was exciting.
Persue	Pursue	"Pursue" sounds like "per-sue," but it only has one 'e' at the end.	I plan to pursue a career in science.
Beleive	Believe	I before E, except after C.	I believe in doing my best every day.
Suprise	Surprise	The "surprise" has an extra 'r' after 'u'.	I love surprises on my birthday.
Occured	Occurred	Double 'r' and 'e' – two 'c's, two 'r's.	The incident occurred during lunch.
Gaurd	Guard	"Guard" starts with "gua," not "gau."	The guard kept watch at the school entrance.
Definate	Definite	"Definite" comes from "finite," meaning certain.	There's a definite chance of rain today.
Supose	Suppose	Think "supposition" to remember the extra 'p'.	I suppose I could help with your project.
Existance	Existence	"Existence" has "exist" + "ence."	The existence of dinosaurs fascinates me.
Untill	Until	Only one 'l' at the end of "until."	We waited until the movie started.

Common spelling and vocabulary errors :

25 common spelling and vocabulary errors frequently made by middle school students .

Common Error	Correct Version	Tip/Trick to Remember	Example Sentence (Correct Usage)
Alot	A lot	"A lot" is two words, not one.	There is a lot of homework to do this weekend.
Definately	Definitely	Think "definite" + "ly" = definitely.	I will definitely go to the party on Saturday.
Seperate	Separate	There's a "rat" in separate.	Keep your school and personal life separate.
Their/There/They're	Their, There, They're	"Their" is possession, "There" is a place, "They're" = they are.	Their house is over there, and they're coming soon.
Your/You're	Your, You're	"Your" is possession, "You're" means "you are."	You're going to need your notebook today.
Its/It's	Its, It's	"Its" is possession, "It's" means "it is."	The dog wagged its tail because it's happy.
Then/Than	Than, Then	"Than" is for comparison; "Then" refers to time.	I am taller than my brother, and then we went to play basketball.
Wich	Which	Remember: "Which" has two 'h's like a "witch on Halloween."	Which book did you borrow from the library?
Recieve	Receive	I before E, except after C.	I was happy to receive the letter from my friend.
Accomodate	Accommodate	"Accommodation" has double 'c' and 'm'.	The hotel will accommodate all guests.
Excercise	Exercise	"Exercise" has "cise" like "scissors" because you cut calories.	I exercise every morning before school.
Febuary	February	"February" has an extra 'r' after 'b'.	February is the shortest month of the year.
Tommorow	Tomorrow	"Tomorrow" has two 'r's, like racing to the future.	Tomorrow, we have a math test.
Wednsday	Wednesday	Break it down: "Wed-nes-day."	Wednesday is the middle of the school week.
Embarras	Embarrass	"Embarrass" has double 'r' and 's' – don't let them embarrass you!	I felt embarrassed when I tripped in front of the class.
Begining	Beginning	Remember: Two 'n's in the middle.	The beginning of the story was exciting.
Persue	Pursue	"Pursue" sounds like "per-sue," but it only has one 'e' at the end.	I plan to pursue a career in science.
Beleive	Believe	I before E, except after C.	I believe in doing my best every day.
Suprise	Surprise	The "surprise" has an extra 'r' after 'u'.	I love surprises on my birthday.
Occured	Occurred	Double 'r' and 'e' – two 'c's, two 'r's.	The incident occurred during lunch.
Gaurd	Guard	"Guard" starts with "gua," not "gau."	The guard kept watch at the school entrance.
Definate	Definite	"Definite" comes from "finite," meaning certain.	There's a definite chance of rain today.
Supose	Suppose	Think "supposition" to remember the extra 'p'.	I suppose I could help with your project.
Existance	Existence	"Existence" has "exist" + "ence."	The existence of dinosaurs fascinates me.
Untill	Until	Only one 'l' at the end of "until."	We waited until the movie started.

Trivia Corner

- The Longest Word Ever Misspelled: The word "antidisestablishmentarianism" is famously long, and students often misspell it due to its complex structure. It's not just a spelling challenge, but a vocabulary one too!

- The "Misspelled" Irony: The word "misspelled" is one of the most commonly misspelled words. The irony is that many students misspell it by adding an extra 's' (missspelled)!

- Shakespeare's Spelling Choices: Even though he was a master of language, William Shakespeare didn't always spell his own name the same way. There are over 80 different spellings of his name found in historical documents!

- The Accidental Space Error: In 1962, a missing hyphen in the computer code caused NASA's Mariner I spacecraft to crash. This simple spelling mistake cost $18 million and is known as one of history's most expensive typos.

- "Their" and "There" Confusion: One of the most common spelling errors made by students is mixing up "their" (possessive), "there" (location), and "they're" (they are). This confusion even happens in professional writing!

- The "i before e" Rule Doesn't Always Apply: While the "i before e except after c" rule is widely taught, there are more than 900 exceptions to this rule, including words like "weird" and "height."

- Silent Letters Were Once Pronounced: Words like "knight" and "gnome" used to be pronounced with the silent letters (e.g., "k" in knight). Over time, English speakers stopped pronouncing these letters, but they remain in the spelling!

- The First Dictionary: The first full English dictionary, compiled by Samuel Johnson in 1755, listed around 40,000 words. Even back then, spelling was not standardized, and Johnson had to make decisions on many spellings that are still used today.

- Autocorrect Fails: While technology helps catch many spelling mistakes, autocorrect isn't always perfect. Sometimes it can turn "duck" into something completely inappropriate, leading to some pretty hilarious and embarrassing typos!

Trivia Corner

- The Most Commonly Misspelled Word in English: According to many surveys, "separate" is the most commonly misspelled word in the English language, with people often writing it as "seperate." Remember, there's "a rat" in "separate" to help you spell it correctly!

- The Most Expensive Typo: In 2006, a company lost $10 million due to a single misplaced comma in a contract. This mistake altered the terms of the deal and resulted in a huge financial loss. Even small punctuation marks matter!

- The Shortest Complete Sentence: The shortest sentence in the English language is "I am." Even though it's only two words, it's grammatically correct and packs a punch in terms of meaning!

- The Word "Clew" Became "Clue": The word "clue" originally came from the word "clew," which referred to a ball of thread. In Greek mythology, Theseus used a clew to find his way out of a labyrinth. Over time, "clew" morphed into "clue," meaning a hint to solve a puzzle.

- Old Spelling of "Potato": In 1992, the then U.S. Vice President Dan Quayle famously corrected a 12-year-old student's spelling of "potato" to "potatoe" during a spelling bee, leading to widespread media coverage. This error became infamous in U.S. political history.

- Double Letters Confusion: Double consonants often confuse students when spelling words like "occurrence" or "recommendation." A good trick for remembering "recommend" is that it contains two "m's" because it's doubly important!

🎯 ACTIVITY CORNER 9

Activity 1: Match the Misspelled Word with Its Correct Spelling

Column A (Incorrect Spelling)	Column B (Options)
1. Acommodate	a) Acomodate b) Accomodate c) Accommodate d) Acomadate
2. Definately	a) Definately b) Defanately c) Definitely d) Definetely
3. Recieve	a) Receive b) Recieve c) Recive d) Reccieve
4. Tommorrow	a) Tommorow b) Tomorrow c) Tomorow d) Tommorrow
5. Seperate	a) Separate b) Seperate c) Sepperate d) Seporate

Activity 2 : Fill in the Blank (Common Vocabulary Mistakes)

Fill in the blank with the correct spelling or word choice:
1. She had to (_____ / there / their) umbrella because it was raining.
2. Please (advise / _____) me about the homework deadline.
3. The dog buried its bone in the (garden / _____).
4. We are going (too / _____) the mall after school.
5. It's (your / _____) turn to wash the dishes.

Activity 3 : Spot the Mistake (Proofreading Paragraph)

Read the paragraph below and circle the 5 spelling and grammar errors:

"John went too the store to buy there favorite snacks. He could'nt find them, so he asked an employee for assitance. The employee reffered him to the correct aisle. He was able to find every snack accept for the chips."

10. Real-World Uses of Spelling and Vocabulary Skills

In this chapter, you will learn how your spelling and vocabulary skills can significantly impact your life, not only in school but also in everyday situations such as writing emails, communicating online, and preparing for your future career. With engaging examples, tables, and practice exercises, you will understand how these skills are valuable tools for success.

How Spelling and Vocabulary Help in School

In school, spelling and vocabulary skills are essential for clear communication. Whether you're writing essays, answering questions in class, or reading, your ability to choose the right words and spell them correctly makes your work more polished and easier to understand.

Example 1: Essay Writing

The word's definition is directly stated. You've been assigned an essay on The Hunger Games. Instead of saying Katniss is "strong" repeatedly, you can use words like "resilient," "determined," and "brave" to describe her character, which will make your writing more impressive.

Table: Replacing Simple Words in Essays

Simple Word	Better Word Choices	Sentence Example
Strong	Powerful, Resilient, Tough	"Katniss was resilient in facing every challenge."
Happy	Delighted, Joyful, Ecstatic	"Peeta was ecstatic when he reunited with Katniss."
Scared	Terrified, Frightened, Apprehensive	"She was apprehensive about entering the arena."
Sad	Heartbroken, Miserable, Despondent	"The district was despondent after the attack."

Practical Applications for Future Success :

Knowing how to use a strong vocabulary and spell words correctly is essential for the future. Having excellent communication skills will set you apart from others when applying for jobs, internships, or college.

Example : Writing a Job Application

Let's say you are applying for a position as a camp counselor. Compare these two versions of a sentence in your application:

Sentence 1: "I am good at working with kids."
Sentence 2: "I excel at engaging with children and fostering a positive environment."

Clearly, the second sentence sounds more professional and highlights your skills better.

Table: Improving Sentences for Job Applications

Simple Sentence	Improved Sentence
I work well with others.	I collaborate effectively with my peers and leaders.
I am responsible.	I take ownership of my tasks and am dependable in any situation.
I helped with activities.	I facilitated engaging activities for children during camp.
I am good at math.	I have strong mathematical skills, particularly in algebra.

Letters, Emails, and Online Communication :

Much of today's communication occurs online. Whether you're sending an email to a teacher or chatting with friends, spelling and vocabulary play a significant role. Writing emails with proper spelling and clear vocabulary demonstrates responsibility and thoughtfulness

Example: Sending an Email

Imagine you need to email your teacher about a missed assignment. Compare these two versions of an email:

Email 1: "Hi Mr. Brown, I missed class today. What did we do?"

Email 2: "Dear Mr. Brown,
I hope you're doing well. Unfortunately, I was unable to attend class today due to illness. Could you please let me know what I missed and if there's anything I should catch up on?
Thank you.
Sincerely,
Lily"

The second email is more polite, uses better vocabulary, and gives a positive impression.

Table: Informal vs. Formal Communication

Informal Phrase	Formal Phrase
Hey	Dear
Can u tell me what we did?	Could you let me know what we covered?
Thx for the help	Thank you for your assistance.
Bye!	Sincerely
Emojis 😊	No emojis in formal writing

Writing Emails and Letters with Proper Vocabulary

Here are a few more activities to help you practice spelling and vocabulary in real-world writing situations.

Activity 1: Peer Email Review

- Write an email to a friend explaining what you did over the weekend.
- Exchange emails with a classmate and review each other's spelling and vocabulary. Suggest improvements!

Activity 2: Word Choice in Letters Rewrite the following sentences using more sophisticated vocabulary:

- "I had fun at the park." (Improve: "I enjoyed my time at the park immensely.")
- "The homework was hard." (Improve: "The homework was challenging but rewarding.")

Activity 3: Word Bank for Professional Writing Create a word bank of 10 strong vocabulary words useful in formal writing (like emails or letters). Then, write a short letter using at least five of those words.

Example Word Bank:
- Appreciate
- Assistance
- Ensure
- Confirm
- Notify

Letter Example:

"Dear Ms. Roberts,
I wanted to express my appreciation for your assistance with the science project. Your feedback helped make sure that I completed the project successfully. Please notify me if there's anything else I can improve.
Best regards,
Aiden"

Activity 4: Match the Mistake. Look at the sentences below and find the vocabulary or spelling mistakes. Then, correct it:

- "Their going to the park after school."
- "I recieved the package yesterday."
- "He is a very inteligent student."

Answers:

- "They're going to the park after school."
- "I received the package yesterday."
- "He is a very intelligent student."

Conclusion

Spelling and vocabulary are important for effective communication in school and beyond. Whether you're writing essays, sending emails, or communicating online, using the right words and spelling them correctly can have a big impact. Keep practicing these skills, and you'll feel more confident in all your writing!

Trivia Corner

- **Fun Fact**: Spellcheck wasn't invented until the 1970s! Before that, people had to rely solely on dictionaries and proofreading.
- **Historical Fact**: One of the most famous spelling mistakes in history happened on the 1885 Statue of Liberty plaque! The word "Future" was misspelled as "Furure."
- **Did you know**? In emails, using clear and professional language increases the chances of getting a positive response by up to 50%.
- **Tech Fact**: Most autocorrect systems use a built-in dictionary of around 60,000 words to help fix spelling mistakes.
- **Career Trivia**: Many job recruiters say that spelling mistakes in job applications are one of the main reasons they reject candidates. Proofreading matters!
- **Fun Fact**: The word "emoji" comes from Japan, and even though it's a symbol, the proper spelling and use of words around emojis are key to communication.
- **Literary Trivia**: Famous author Mark Twain said, "Anyone who can only think of one way to spell a word obviously lacks imagination!" He believed spelling wasn't as rigid as grammar.
- **Did you know**? In text messaging, even with abbreviations like "LOL" and "BRB," spelling correctly is still considered important in formal communications like emailing your teacher or principal.
- **Fun Fact**: The word "quiz" was allegedly created in 1791 by a Dublin theater manager who made a bet that he could introduce a new word into the English language in just 48 hours!

ACTIVITY CORNER 10

Activity 1: Match the Correct Word with its Definition (Vocabulary in Emails and Letters)

Word	Definition
1. Professional	a. A casual greeting at the start of a letter/email
2. Salutation	b. A courteous phrase used to close a message
3. Recipient	c. The person receiving the letter or email
4. Closing	d. Maintaining a formal tone and correct language usage

Activity 2 : Fill in the Blank (Using the Right Vocabulary in Real-World Writing)

Complete the sentences with the correct word from the word bank.

Word Bank: *respectfully, sincerely, informal, formal, recipient*

1. When writing a letter to your principal, use a _____ tone.
2. Always end a professional email with "_____" or "best regards."
3. An email to a close friend can be _____ and casual.
4. The person you're sending the email to is called the _____.
5. To show politeness in writing, start with "Dear" and end with "_____."

Activity 3 : Substitute with a Better Word (Avoiding Repetitive Words)

In each sentence, replace the bold word with a better synonym from the word bank.
Word Bank: effective, delighted, assistance, respond, important

1. I was really **happy** to receive your email.
2. Please **reply** to my email by tomorrow.
3. Your help with this project was very **helpful**.
4. It's **important** to proofread your emails.
5. Thank you for your **help** on this task.

ACTIVITY ANSWERS

ACTIVITY CORNER 1

Activity 1: Spelling Challenge

Answers:
1. The **receipt** for the project was not ready.
2. She had **definitely** planned to attend the **committee** meeting.
3. The **environment** club helped clean the park.

Activity 2: Choose the correct word

1. The decision did not **affect** the outcome.
2. Please **accept** my apology for the delay.
3. **They're** going to the park later this evening.

Activity 3: Homophones Match-Up activity

Words	Correct Match
Principal	B
Principle	D
Complement	C
Compliment	A
Affect	E
Effect	F

Activity 4: Match the Word to the Correct Meaning

Vocabulary Answer

a) Unavoidable
b) Exact
a) Sudden change
a) Tiny particle

ACTIVITY CORNER 2

ACTIVITY 1: MULTIPLE-CHOICE QUIZ

1. b) Threatening
2. c) Very happy
3. b) Hardworking

ACTIVITY 2 : MATCH THE FOLLOWING

1. b) Before
2. c) Not
3. a) Full of
4. d) Without

ACTIVITY CORNER 3: TRUE OR FALSE

1. a) True
2. a) True
3. b) False

ACTIVITY CORNER 4 : VOCABULARY CHALLENGE - MATCH THE WORD WITH ITS DEFINITION

1. c) Exact
2. a) Unable to be avoided
3. b) Very small particle
4. d) Sudden and major change

ACTIVITY CORNER 3

ACTIVITY 1: TRUE OR FALSE - SPELLING RULES

Answers:
1. True
2. False (It's "boxes.")
3. True
4. True
5. False (It follows the rule.)

ACTIVITY 2: MATCH THE FOLLOWING - SILENT LETTERS

Answers:
- Knight → K
- Write → W
- Doubt → B
- Hour → H
- Castle → T

ACTIVITY 3: MULTIPLE CHOICE - COMMON SPELLING CHALLENGES

Answers:
1. b) Separate
2. c) Buses
3. c) Definitely

ACTIVITY 4 : FIX THE MISTAKES

Answers:
1. Neighbor
2. Business
3. Rhythm

ACTIVITY CORNER 4

ACTIVITY 1: SYNONYM MATCHING

Answers:
1. Happy → c) Delighted
2. Big → b) Enormous
3. Angry → a) Furious
4. Quiet → d) Silent
5. Fast → e) Quick

ACTIVITY 2: ANTONYM CHALLENGE

Answers:
1. b) Freezing
2. b) Dark
3. a) Soft
4. b) Sad
5. b) Quiet

ACTIVITY 3: HOMONYM HUNT

Answers:
1. there
2. they're
3. hear
4. to
5. its

ACTIVITY 4: FILL IN THE BLANKS (CONTEXT CLUES)

Answers:
1. excited
2. sprinted
3. furious
4. whispered
5. gigantic

ACTIVITY 5: VOCABULARY IN SENTENCES

Answers:
1. a) exhausted
2. b) mysterious
3. a) hot
4. b) clear

ACTIVITY CORNER 5

Activity 1: Context Clues Challenge

Answers:
1. Agile – Quick and light in movement
2. Captivating – Holding the attention, fascinating
3. Drastic – Severe or extreme
4. Exemplary – Outstanding, a model to be followed
5. Intricate – Very detailed and complex

Activity 2: Match the Synonym

1. Jovial – C. Cheerful
2. Ominous – D. Threatening
3. Gracious – B. Kind
4. Tedious – A. Boring
5. Abrupt – E. Sudden

Activity 3: Word Detective

1. Luminous – Bright, glowing
2. Serene – Calm, peaceful
3. Rustling – Soft, crackling noise
4. Aromatic – Pleasant-smelling
5. Tranquility – A state of peace and quiet

Activity 4: Fill in the Blanks

1. Immaculate
2. Plausible
3. Majestic
4. Captivating
5. Tedious

Activity 5 : Create a Sentence

- The dark clouds in the distance looked ominous, and we knew a storm was coming.
- The luminous moon lit up the entire beach, making it look magical.
- His jovial laugh made everyone in the room smile.
- The serene lake was the perfect place to relax and read a book.
- It seemed plausible that she had finished the puzzle, considering how quickly she worked.

ACTIVITY CORNER 6

ACTIVITY 1: WORD ROOTS QUIZ

Answer:

1. PHOTO (Greek root meaning "light")
2. SCRIPT (Latin root meaning "to write")
3. AUTO (Prefix meaning "self")
4. OLOGY (Suffix meaning "study of")
5. PRE (Prefix meaning "before")

ACTIVITY 2 : MATCH THE PREFIX AND MEANING

Answer:

1. Anti- = B. Against
2. Sub- = D. Under
3. Hyper- = E. Over, excessive
4. Post- = A. After
5. Re- = C. Again

ACTIVITY 3 : CREATE WORDS FROM ROOTS

1. Spect + -acle = Spectacle
2. Dict + Pre- = Predict
3. Form + Re- = Reform
4. Port + Ex- = Export
5. Act + -ion = Action

ACTIVITY 4 : IDENTIFY THE ROOT AND ITS MEANING

1) Biology
- Root: "bio"
- Meaning: "life"

2) Transport
- Root: "port"
- Meaning: "carry"

3) Autograph
- Root: "auto"
- Meaning: "self"

4) Predict
- Root: "dict"
- Meaning: "speak" or "say"

5) Photograph
- Root: "photo"
- Meaning: "light"

6) Television
- Root: "tele"
- Meaning: "far" or "distant"

7) Construct
- Root: "struct"
- Meaning: "build"

8) Thermometer
- Root: "thermo"
- Meaning: "heat"

9) Hydrate
- Root: "hydr"
- Meaning: "water"

10) Manual
- Root: "man"
- Meaning: "hand"

ACTIVITY CORNER 7

ACTIVITY 1 : UNSCRAMBLE THE WORDS

Answers:

1. definitely
2. occurrence
3. restaurant
4. recommend
5. programming

ACTIVITY 2 : UNSCRAMBLE THE WORDS

Answers:

1. They're
2. Your
3. There
4. You're
5. Their

ACTIVITY 3 : FILL-IN-THE-BLANK SPELLING

Answers:

1. The teacher will recommend the best book for you to read.
2. I will sign the letter with my name at the end.
3. It is necessary to study for your spelling test.
4. She felt a lot of excitement when she saw her friends.
5. The dog was disappointed that he didn't get a treat.

ACTIVITY 4: MATCH THE WORD FROM THE LEFT COLUMN WITH ITS CORRECT DEFINITION FROM THE RIGHT COLUMN.

Answers:

1. Guarantee → b. A promise that something will happen
2. Privilege → c. A special right or advantage
3. Recommend → a. A strong recommendation
4. Accommodate → d. Make room or space for something
5. Intelligence → e. The ability to acquire and apply knowledge

ACTIVITY CORNER 8

ACTIVITY 1:
MATCH THE FOLLOWING

Answer Key:
1. Big — b) Massive
2. Small — c) Tiny
3. Happy — d) Elated
4. Sad — e) Melancholy
5. Surprising — a) Astonishing

ACTIVITY 2:
CHOOSE THE CORRECT OPTION

Answer Key:

1. Friendly
2. Precision
3. Mysterious
4. Exhausted
5. Extensive

ACTIVITY 3:
FILL IN THE BLANK

Answer Key:

1. Radiant
2. Anxious
3. Enormous
4. Fascinated
5. Swift

ACTIVITY 4: SUBSTITUTE WITH A BETTER WORD

Answers:

1. The movie was hilarious.
2. The rollercoaster ride was terrifying.
3. Winning the championship was a crucial moment for the team.
4. Her performance in the play was exceptional.
5. The fireworks display on the Fourth of July was spectacular.

ACTIVITY 5: SYNONYM SEARCH - FIND BETTER WORDS

Answers:

1. The cake was delicious.
2. He felt guilty after the argument.
3. The view from the mountain was breathtaking.
4. The book was fascinating.
5. She was furious at her brother for breaking her toy.

ACTIVITY CORNER 9

ACTIVITY 1 : MATCH THE MISSPELLED WORD WITH ITS CORRECT SPELLING

Answers:

1. Accommodate
2. Definitely
3. Receive
4. Tomorrow
5. Separate

ACTIVITY 2 : FILL IN THE BLANK (COMMON VOCABULARY MISTAKES)

Answers:

1. their
2. advice
3. garden
4. to
5. your

ACTIVITY 3 : SPOT THE MISTAKE (PROOFREADING PARAGRAPH)

Answers:

1. too → to
2. there → their
3. could'nt → couldn't
4. assitance → assistance
5. accept → except

ACTIVITY CORNER 10

ACTIVITY 1: MATCH THE CORRECT WORD WITH ITS DEFINITION

Answers:

1 - d, 2 - a, 3 - c, 4 - b

ACTIVITY 3 : SUBSTITUTE WITH A BETTER WORD

Answers:

1. delighted
2. respond
3. effective
4. important (no change)
5. assistance

ACTIVITY 2 : FILL IN THE BLANK

Answers:

1. formal
2. sincerely
3. informal
4. recipient
5. respectfully

11. Build Your Word Bank: Vocabulary Essentials

TABLE: VOCABULARY IMPROVEMENT GROUPS

GROUP 1: WORDS FROM LATIN ROOTS

Word	Breakdown	Meaning	Tip to Remember
Amicable	Amic (friend)	Friendly	Think of "Amic" like "Amiable," both mean friendly.
Belligerent	Bell (war)	Hostile, Aggressive	"Bell" sounds like "Battle," which means fighting.
Benefactor	Bene (good)	Someone who helps others	"Bene" means good, like benefit (something good).
Malediction	Male (bad)	Curse	"Male" means bad, opposite of "Bene" (good).
Magnanimous	Magn (great)	Generous	"Magn" means great, think of a magnifying glass that makes things bigger.
Veracity	Ver (truth)	Truthfulness	"Ver" is like verify, which means to check the truth.
Precipitate	Pre (before)	Cause to happen suddenly	"Pre" means before, like when something happens quickly.
Incredulous	In (not) + Cred (believe)	Skeptical	"Cred" means believe, and "in" means not—so, not believing.
Equanimity	Equ (equal)	Calmness	"Equ" means equal or balanced, like equal feelings.
Obdurate	Ob (against) + Dur (hard)	Stubborn	"Dur" is like durable, meaning tough or hard to change.

Examples:

- **Amicable**: "Our discussion was very amicable; no one got angry."
- **Belligerent**: "The player was belligerent on the field, always looking for a fight."
- **Benefactor**: "The school's new library was donated by a generous benefactor."
- **Malediction**: "The wizard cast a terrible malediction on the village."
- **Magnanimous**: "Even though he lost the game, he was magnanimous and congratulated the winner."
- **Veracity**: "The reporter was known for her veracity, always telling the truth."
- **Precipitate**: "The sudden storm precipitated our decision to leave early."
- **Incredulous**: "She was incredulous when she heard she had won the lottery."
- **Equanimity**: "Despite the chaos, she maintained her equanimity and stayed calm."
- **Obdurate**: "No matter how much they argued, he remained obdurate and refused to change his mind."

VOCABULARY IMPROVEMENT GROUPS
GROUP 2: WORDS FROM GREEK ROOTS

Word	Breakdown	Meaning	Tip to Remember
Chronology	Chron (time) + -logy (study of)	Study of time or events in order	"Chron" sounds like "chronological order" (how things happen in time).
Democracy	Demo (people) + -cracy (government)	Government by the people	"Demo" means people, like in democracy, where people have power.
Philosophy	Philo (love) + -sophy (wisdom)	Love of wisdom or knowledge	"Philo" means love, and "sophy" means wisdom. Think of wise thinking.
Autonomy	Auto (self) + -nomy (law)	Self-governance or independence	"Auto" means self—like a car that moves by itself. Auto-law means making your own rules.
Apathetic	A (not) + path (feeling)	Not caring or indifferent	"Path" means feeling, so "a-path-etic" means no feelings.
Kaleidoscope	Kaleido (beautiful) + scope (view)	A constantly changing pattern	"Kaleido" means beautiful, and "scope" means to see—like seeing beautiful patterns.
Homogeneous	Homo (same) + -geneous (kind)	Of the same kind	"Homo" means same—like in homogeneous where everything is similar.
Hypothesis	Hypo (under) + thesis (proposition)	A proposed explanation	"Hypo" means under, and "thesis" is an idea—so, it's an educated guess.
Metamorphosis	Meta (change) + morph (form)	Transformation or big change	"Meta" means change, and "morph" means form—like butterflies going through metamorphosis.
Bibliophile	Biblio (book) + -phile (lover)	A book lover	"Biblio" means book, and "phile" means lover—someone who loves books.

Examples:

- **Chronology**: "We learned the chronology of events that led to the Civil War."
- **Democracy**: "In a democracy, people vote to choose their leaders."
- **Philosophy**: "His philosophy is that everyone should help one another."
- **Autonomy:** "The country gained autonomy after fighting for its independence."
- **Apathetic**: "She was apathetic about the school dance and didn't want to go."
- **Kaleidoscope**: "Looking through the kaleidoscope, we saw beautiful patterns and colors."
- **Homogeneous:** "The students in the class were homogeneous because they all wore the same uniform."
- **Hypothesis**: "The scientist made a hypothesis about how the plants would grow."
- **Metamorphosis**: "The caterpillar went through metamorphosis and became a butterfly."
- **Bibliophile**: "As a bibliophile, she spends all her free time reading books."

VOCABULARY IMPROVEMENT GROUPS

GROUP 3: WORDS WITH POSITIVE CONNOTATIONS

Word	Breakdown	Meaning	Tip to Remember
Benevolent	Bene (good) + volent (wishing)	Kind-hearted	"Bene" means good—think of being kind.
Exuberant	Ex (out) + uber (fruitful)	Joyfully energetic	"Ex" means out, like overflowing with energy.
Magnanimous	Magn (great) + animous (spirit)	Generous	"Magn" means great—like magnify, making something bigger, including kindness.
Serendipity	Ser (serene) + dipity (finding)	Finding happiness by chance	"Ser" is like serene, or finding unexpected happiness.
Jubilant	Jubil (shout for joy)	Extremely joyful	"Jubil" sounds like jubilee, a big celebration.
Altruistic	Altru (other) + istic (quality)	Selflessly helping others	"Altru" means others—think about helping others first.
Felicitous	Felic (happy)	Well-suited or pleasant	"Felic" sounds like felicity, which means happiness.
Ebullient	E (out) + bulli (boil)	Cheerfully enthusiastic	"Ebull" sounds like bubble, like bubbling with joy.
Amicable	Amic (friend)	Friendly	"Amic" sounds like amiable, meaning friendly.
Sanguine	Sanguin (blood)	Optimistic	"Sanguin" means blood—think rosy cheeks and happiness.

Examples:

- **Benevolent**: "The benevolent teacher always helped students who were struggling."
- **Exuberant:** "She was so exuberant at the party, dancing and laughing all night."
- **Magnanimous**: "His magnanimous gesture of donating books to the school was appreciated."
- **Serendipity**: "It was serendipity when they found a lost puppy that turned out to belong to their neighbor."
- **Jubilant:** "The team was jubilant after winning the championship game."
- **Altruistic:** "Her altruistic nature showed when she spent weekends volunteering."
- **Felicitous**: "His felicitous choice of words made the speech perfect."
- **Ebullient:** "Her ebullient personality always cheered up her friends."
- **Amicable:** "Even though they disagreed, they remained amicable and worked things out."
- **Sanguine**: "He had a sanguine outlook, always believing things would turn out okay."

VOCABULARY IMPROVEMENT GROUPS

GROUP 4: WORDS WITH NEGATIVE CONNOTATIONS

Word	Breakdown	Meaning	Tip to Remember
Malevolent	Male (bad) + volent (wishing)	Evil-minded	"Male" means bad—think of someone with bad intentions.
Ominous	Omin (omen) + -ous (full of)	Threatening	"Omin" sounds like omen, meaning a bad sign.
Vindictive	Vindict (revenge) + -ive (quality)	Revengeful	"Vindict" sounds like convict, someone seeking revenge.
Nefarious	Nefar (evil) + -ious (full of)	Wicked	"Nefar" sounds like nefarious, meaning really bad.
Pernicious	Per (thoroughly) + nic (harm) + -ious (full of)	Harmful	"Nic" sounds like noxious, which means harmful.
Egregious	E (out) + greg (flock) + -ious (full of)	Outrageously bad	"Greg" means flock, but this is someone standing out in a bad way.
Deleterious	Deleter (harmful) + -ious (full of)	Harmful	"Delete" sounds like to remove, which has a harmful effect.
Invidious	In (against) + vid (see) + -ious (full of)	Envious	"Invid" sounds like envy, someone who causes harm by being jealous.
Recalcitrant	Re (back) + calcitr (kicking) + -ant (quality)	Stubbornly resistant	"Calci" sounds like calcify, which means hardened or difficult to change.
Insolent	In (not) + solent (customary)	Disrespectful	"Sole" sounds like alone, someone acting rudely or disrespectfully.

Examples:

- **Malevolent:** "The villain in the movie was truly malevolent, always planning something evil."
- **Ominous:** "The dark clouds looked ominous, like a big storm was coming."
- **Vindictive**: "Her vindictive actions showed she wasn't ready to forgive."
- **Nefarious:** "The pirate had a nefarious plan to steal the treasure."
- **Pernicious:** "The pernicious rumor caused a lot of harm in the school."
- **Egregious:** "His egregious behavior in class got him in serious trouble."
- **Deleterious**: "Too much screen time can have a deleterious effect on your sleep."
- **Invidious:** "Her invidious comments made everyone feel uncomfortable."
- **Recalcitrant:** "The recalcitrant student refused to follow the teacher's instructions."
- **Insolent**: "The insolent remark was disrespectful to the teacher."

VOCABULARY IMPROVEMENT GROUPS

GROUP 5: ACADEMIC WORDS

Word	Breakdown	Meaning	Tip to Remember	Similar Words
Hypothesis	Hypo- (under) + thesis (idea)	A guess or idea	"Hypo" means under, "thesis" is an idea	Theory, Assumption
Analyze	Ana- (up) + lyze (break apart)	Study something closely	"Ana" means up, breaking things into parts	Examine, Evaluate
Synthesize	Syn- (together) + thesize (put together)	Combine ideas	"Syn" means together, putting things together	Combine, Merge
Evaluate	E- (out) + valu (value) + ate (make)	Judge the worth	"Valu" means worth, deciding how valuable something is	Judge, Assess
Interpret	Inter- (between) + pret (explain)	Explain the meaning	"Inter" means between, explaining how things connect	Explain, Clarify
Formulate	Form- (shape) + ulate (make)	Create a plan	"Form" means shape, making a detailed plan	Create, Plan
Corroborate	Cor- (together) + robor (strength) + ate (make)	Confirm something	"Robor" means strength, confirming something with evidence	Confirm, Support
Conceptualize	Concept- (idea) + ualize (make)	Form an idea	"Concept" means idea, forming a new idea	Envision, Imagine
Critique	Crit- (judge) + ique (process)	Give a detailed opinion	"Crit" sounds like critic, giving a judgment	Review, Assess
Infer	In- (into) + fer (carry)	Figure out from clues	"Infer" means to guess or figure out from clues	Deduce, Conclude

MOST USED ROOT WORDS FROM DIFFERENT LANGUAGES

TABLE 1: LATIN ROOTS

Root	Meaning	Examples
Aqua	Water	Aquarium, Aquatic, Waterfall
Aud	Hear	Audience, Audible, Hearable
Bene	Good	Benefit, Helpful, Kind
Dict	Say, Speak	Dictate, Dictionary, Speak
Duc/Duct	Lead	Conduct, Educate, Lead
Form	Shape	Formation, Transform, Shape
Ject	Throw	Eject, Inject, Throw
Port	Carry	Transport, Portable, Carry
Rupt	Break	Interrupt, Break, Rupture
Spect	Look	Inspect, Spectator, Watch
Struct	Build	Construct, Structure, Build

TABLE 2: GREEK ROOTS

Root	Meaning	Examples
Chron	Time	Chronology, Timer, Chronic
Dem	People	Democracy, Population, Epidemic
Philo	Love	Philosophy, Book Lover, Friendship
Auto	Self	Autograph, Car, Self-Driving
Hypo	Under	Hypothesis, Under-Skin, Cold (Hypothermia)
Morph	Form	Metamorphosis, Changing Shape, Morph
Therm	Heat	Thermometer, Warm, Heating System
Path	Feeling	Empathy, Sympathy, Pathos
Bio	Life	Biology, Life Story, Biodegradable
Geo	Earth	Geography, Study of Rocks, Ground Heat (Geothermal)

MOST USED ROOT WORDS FROM DIFFERENT LANGUAGES

TABLE 3: FRENCH AND SANSKRIT ROOTS

Root	Language	Meaning	Examples
Café	French	Coffee	Café, Cafeteria
Château	French	Castle	Château, Large House
Ballet	French	Dance	Ballet, Dancer (Ballerina)
Avatar	Sanskrit	Descent (Taking Form)	Avatar, Character (in Games)
Karma	Sanskrit	Action	Karma, Effects of Actions
Nirvana	Sanskrit	Freedom (from Worry)	Nirvana, Peaceful Feeling
Yoga	Sanskrit	Union (Mind & Body)	Yoga, Exercise Practice
Guru	Sanskrit	Teacher	Guru, Wise Leader
Mantra	Sanskrit	Sacred Saying	Mantra, Repeated Phrase
Chakra	Sanskrit	Energy Center (Wheel)	Chakra, Energy Point in Body

TABLE 4 : GERMAN ROOTS

Root	Meaning	Examples
Zeit	Time	Zeitgeist, Zeitgeber
Kinder	Children	Kindergarten, Kindergeld
Haus	House	House, Hausfrau
Arbeit	Work	Arbeit, Arbeitskraft
Geist	Spirit, Mind	Zeitgeist, Poltergeist
Sturm	Storm	Sturm und Drang, Stormtrooper
Wald	Forest	Walden, Waldheim

TABLE 5 : OLD ENGLISH ROOTS

Root	Meaning	Examples
Cyning	King	King, Kingdom
Mann	Person, Human	Man, Woman, Mankind
Hús	House	House, Husband
Frēond	Friend	Friend, Friendship
Folc	People	Folk, Folklore
Scip	Ship	Ship, Skipper

12. Most Misspelled Words & Tricks to Remember

MOST MISSPELLED WORDS BY MIDDLE SCHOOL STUDENTS

Common Word	Mistake	Tip to Remember
Definitely	Definately	"It's definitely not 'definatley'—there's an 'i' in it!"
Separate	Seperate	"A rat is in the middle of 'separate'!"
Accommodate	Accomodate	"Two 'c's and two 'm's make room for everyone!"
Embarrass	Embarass	"If you're embarrassed, remember to double the 'r's and 's's!"
February	Febuary	"Don't forget that 'r'—it's in there, hiding!"
Occurrence	Occurence	"An occurrence has two 'r's and two 'c's, just like it sounds!"
Receive	Recieve	"I before E, except after C—don't let this one deceive!"
Maintenance	Maintanence	"The 'a' is like a main event, but the 'e' keeps it balanced!"
A lot	Alot	"A lot is two words; think of it like 'a whole lot' of fun!"
Misspell	Mispell	"Misspell means to spell 'miss' twice—don't skip the 's'!"
Believed	Beliveed	"I before E, but it's 'believed', not 'beliveed'!"
Friend	Freind	"The 'r' and 'i' are best buds in 'friend'!"
Occasion	Occassion	"Double the 'c' for a special occasion!"
Government	Goverment	"It's 'government' with an 'n' in the middle!"
Guarantee	Guarentee	"A guarantee has a 'u' and a 'tee'—just like a promise!"
Argument	Argumant	"Don't drop the 'e'—keep it strong in 'argument'!"
Calendar	Calender	"Remember, a calendar has an 'a' to keep the days!"
Independence	Independance	"You need an 'e' in 'independence' to be truly free!"
Occurring	Occuring	"Two 'c's make it sound right in 'occurring'!"
Experience	Experiance	"Experience has an 'e' after the 'i'—don't forget it!"
Necessary	Necesary	"You need 'one collar and two sleeves' in 'necessary'!"
Separate	Seperate	"There's a rat in 'separate'—remember the 'a' and 'e'!"
Recommend	Reccommend	"Double the 'c' and the 'm' in 'recommend'—it's a good idea!"
Tomorrow	Tommorrow	"There's only one 'm' in 'tomorrow'—it's coming soon!"
Cemetery	Cemetary	"Cemeteries need a 'e' for peace—remember it!"
Rhythm	Rythm	"Rhythm has a 'y' for the beat—don't forget it!"
Vocabulary	Vocablary	"There's a 'u' in 'vocabulary'—it's key to words!"
Address	Adddress	"Double the 'd's for a perfect address!"
Chocolate	Choclate	"Don't forget the 'o' in chocolate—it's too sweet to miss!"
Liaison	Liason	"A liaison connects with an 'i'—don't drop it!"
Rhythm	Rythym	"There's a 'y' in 'rhythm' for the flow!"
Bureau	Bureu	"Don't forget the 'au' in 'bureau'—it's like a French word!"
Leisure	Lesiure	"Leisure is all about 'ease'—remember it's spelled right!"
Pharaoh	Faraoh	"Pharaoh has 'ph'—just like phone!"
Receipt	Reciept	"'I' comes before 'e' in 'receipt' after the 'c'!"
Environment	Enviroment	"There's an 'n' in 'environment'—nature needs it!"
Minuscule	Miniscule	"It's 'minuscule', not 'miniscule'—think small!"
Possession	Posession	"Two 's's in possession—think of what you own!"

Vacuum	Vacum	"Two 'u's make a clean vacuum!"
Conscious	Conscience	"You need a 'science' to be 'conscious'!"
Tendency	Tendancy	"A tendency has an 'e' to keep it steady!"
Acquaintance	Acquaintence	"There's a 'u' and 'c' in 'acquaintance'—it's all about knowing!"
Parallel	Paralel	"Two 'l's in parallel—like train tracks!"
Dilemma	Dilemna	"A dilemma has two 'm's—choose wisely!"
Acknowledge	Aknowlege	"Don't forget the 'c' in 'acknowledge'—it's key to knowing!"
Restaurateur	Restaurent	"'Restaurateur' is fancy for a restaurant owner—remember the 't'!"
Debris	Debree	"Debris can be tricky—remember it's 'debris', not 'debrie'!"
Questionnaire	Questionare	"It's 'questionnaire' with an extra 'n' for good measure!"
Maneuver	Manuever	"Maneuver has an 'a' and an 'u'—think of a careful move!"
Existence	Existance	"Don't drop the 'e'—existence is key!"

We'd Love Your Feedback!

Please let us know how we're doing by leaving us a review.

CONCLUSION

Congratulations on completing the **Middle School Spelling and Vocabulary Workbook!**

You've embarked on an exciting journey to enhance your spelling and vocabulary skills, and we hope you've enjoyed every step along the way.

As you've explored the chapters, you've learned not just the rules and tricks to spell words correctly but also the importance of a rich vocabulary.

From understanding the nuances of words to practicing them in various contexts, you've built a strong foundation that will serve you well in your academic endeavors and beyond.

Key Takeaways:

1. **Practice Makes Perfect**: Remember, the more you practice, the better you become. Use the exercises and activities in this workbook as a stepping stone to reinforce your skills.
2. **Use Your Vocabulary:** Challenge yourself to use new words in your daily conversations and writing. This will help you remember them and make your communication more effective and expressive.
3. **Make It Fun**: Spelling and vocabulary learning can be exciting! Engage in games, quizzes, and discussions with friends and family to keep the learning alive.
4. **Never Stop Learning:** Language is always evolving, and there's always more to learn. Keep exploring new words, reading widely, and challenging yourself to grow your language skills.

A Word of Encouragement:

As you continue your educational journey, remember that mastering spelling and vocabulary is a gradual process. Mistakes are part of learning, so embrace them as opportunities to improve. Celebrate your progress, no matter how small, and keep striving for excellence.

Thank you for choosing this workbook to enhance your spelling and vocabulary skills. We hope it has been a valuable resource for you. Keep shining, and continue to embrace the beauty of language!
Happy learning!

APPENDIX- 1 : ADDITIONAL RESOURCES

Recommended Books

Title	Author	Description
Word Power Made Easy	Norman Lewis	A comprehensive vocabulary-building book.
The Elements of Style	Strunk and White	A classic guide to effective writing and grammar.
Vocabulary for the High School Student	Harold Levine, Norman Levine, and Robert T. Levine	A book focused on vocabulary development for high school students.
The Vocabulary Builder Workbook	Chris Lele	Engaging activities and exercises for vocabulary growth.
Webster's New World Essential Vocabulary	David A Herzog	A guide to expanding your vocabulary with essential words.

Recommended Websites

Website	URL	Description
Merriam-Webster Dictionary	www.merriam-webster.com	Online dictionary and thesaurus with word games and quizzes.
Vocabulary.com	www.vocabulary.com	Personalized vocabulary practice and games.
Quizlet	www.quizlet.com	Flashcards and learning tools for various subjects, including vocabulary.
Grammarly Blog	www.grammarly.com/blog	Articles on writing, grammar, and vocabulary improvement.
BBC Learning English	www.bbc.co.uk/learningenglish	English language learning resources and vocabulary exercises.

APPENDIX-1 : ADDITIONAL RESOURCES

Recommended Apps

App	Platform	Description
Duolingo	iOS, Android	Language learning app with vocabulary practice.
Anki	iOS, Android	Flashcard app that helps with memorization.
Memrise	iOS, Android	Language and vocabulary learning app with interactive courses.
WordUp Vocabulary	iOS, Android	App that helps you learn new words through games and quizzes.
Vocabulary.com	iOS, Android	App version of the website with personalized vocabulary practice.

We'd Love Your Feedback!

Please let us know how we're doing by leaving us a review.

APPENDIX- 2: WRITING PROMPTS TO USE NEW VOCABULARY IN CONTEXT

Prompt	Description
Describe Your Perfect Day	Write about your perfect day and use at least five new vocabulary words. Be colorful in your descriptions to help your reader imagine your fun day!
A Special Memory	Think about a special memory from your life. Write about it using at least five vocabulary words from the workbook to make your story more exciting!
Persuasive Letter	Choose something you really care about and write a persuasive letter to someone (like a teacher or parent) using at least seven new vocabulary words to share your opinion. Possible topics could be school lunches, favorite activities, or sports.
Create a Short Story	Write a short story (at least 500 words) about anything you enjoy—like a mystery, adventure, or even a day in the life of a student—while using at least ten new vocabulary words.
Letter to a Friend	Write a letter to a friend about something cool you've learned or experienced recently. Use at least five vocabulary words to make it fun and interesting!
Debate Prep	Get ready for a debate! Write a paragraph for your opening statement on a topic you care about, using at least five new vocabulary words to make your point clear.
News Report	Pretend you are a journalist! Write a news article about something exciting that happened recently or a topic you find interesting. Use at least seven vocabulary words to sound professional!
Descriptive Paragraph	Describe a place you've visited or want to visit. Use at least five new vocabulary words to help your reader picture the scene.
Poem or Song Lyrics	Write a poem or some song lyrics using at least five new vocabulary words. Think about how these words help paint a picture or show feelings in your writing.
Dream Big	Write about your dreams and goals for the future. Use at least five vocabulary words to explain what you want to achieve and how you plan to do it.

YOUNG WRITER SERIES - DR. FANATOMY

www.ingramcontent.com/pod-product-compliance
Lightning Source LLC
Chambersburg PA
CBHW082210070526
44585CB00020B/2353